MW01640164

ROADS TO IVY LEAGUE COLLEGES

ROADS TO IVY LEAGUE COLLEGES

Edited by Doris G. Wang

ABAVIEW Publishing

Atlanta

Published in the United States of America
By ABAVIEW Publishing
www.abaview.com

ABAVIEW Publishing
P.O. Box 98155
Atlanta, GA 30359-8155 USA

A catalogue record of this book will be available.
ISBN-10: 098431380X (pb)
ISBN-13: 978098431380x (pb)

Cover designed by Robert W. Fu

First edition
Printed in the United States of America
By Rose Printing Company, Inc.

CONTENTS

Preface

The term Ivy League was originally used to describe an athletic conference that comprised eight private institutions of higher education: Brown University, Columbia University, Cornell University, Dartmouth College, Harvard University, Princeton University, the University of Pennsylvania, and Yale University. These Ivy League universities are located in the Northeastern United States. All of the Ivy League schools, or Ivies, are consistently placed at or near the top in various national and international academic rankings. The term Ivy League now symbolizes academic excellence, selectivity, prestige, and success.

To go to an Ivy League college is the dream of many high school students throughout the world. Some students, like the contributors in this book, have made this dream a reality, while others are still working hard to achieve this goal. Although the Ivy League students featured in this book have different social, economic, and academic backgrounds, the roads they took to the Ivies share some commonalities which are reflected in their activities and essays. This book presents original records of these students as they marched from their high schools towards Ivy League campuses.

This book is divided into eight sections, arranged in alphabetical order by the eight Ivy League colleges. Each section begins with a brief information page about the University provided by the section editor and is followed by individual chapters contributed by selected Ivy League students. As a major component of each chapter, a student's high school accomplishments and extra-curricular activities are provided. Numbers in parenthesis such as (9 - 12) indicate the high school year(s) these events occurred. These extra-curricular activities during their high school are certainly important in defining who they are, in addition to their excellent academic scores that the book did not include. At the end of each chapter, the original essay that each contributor submitted for college application is presented without any editing. Twenty-seven essays tell twenty-seven different touching stories that reflect the interesting, dynamic, and unique life experience of the authors, not only as young learners, but also as members of society.

"Roads to Ivy League Colleges" highlights the pre-college activities of a tiny fraction of Ivy League students with Chinese cultural heritage. Different readers may find it valuable in different ways based on their own perspective. For example, some students may be able to relate these activities to their own pursuits and college choices. Educators from different cultural backgrounds may get a sense of what high school students in America are doing as they prepare for college. Scholars of Chinese American studies may find this book a valuable primary resource in support of their research. Some others may purely enjoy reading these thoughtful essays. These essays, written by Ivy League college-longing high school students, not only serve as a testimony of their inspiration and drive, but may also serve as sample essays for future college applicants. This collection illustrates roads some have taken to Ivy League campuses. I hope that these cases can stimulate your imagination to draw your own map to reach your dream college, which will be the true measure of success for this book.

Finally, I would like to thank section editors for their enthusiasm and diligent work and contributors for sharing their invaluable experience with the world. It has truly been my joy working with such a group of bright and engaging young learners. To all the contributors, I wish you an unparalleled career success ahead propelled by your Ivy League education.

Doris G. Wang

Atlanta

ROADS TO IVY LEAGUE COLLEGES

SECTION I **BROWN UNIVERSITY**

Official Name:	Brown University
Location:	Providence, Rhode Island
Website:	http://www.brown.edu
Year established:	1764
Founder:	John Brown
Motto:	*In Deo speramus* ("In God We Hope")
Mascot:	Bruno the bear
Colors:	Seal brown, cardinal red, and white

Undergraduate student population:	5,851 (2008)
Freshmen population:	1,548 (Fall, 2008)
Domestic students	88%
International students	12%

Colleges on campus:

The College of Brown University
Brown University Graduate School
Warren Alpert Medical School

Section editor: Ivana H. Miao

Ivana H. Miao

From Northview to Brown

High School

Northview High School
10625 Parsons Road
Johns Creek, GA 30097

Population of Graduating
Class: 538

Students to Ivy
League Colleges that Year:
10

Extra-curricular Activities During High School

Music/Arts

- Dance (12 years)
  - Atlanta Professional Dance School (9-12)
    Trained at the Pre-Professional Level in Ballet, Chinese folk dance, and Modern dance
  - Atlanta Ballet (9-10)
    Selected by auditions to train and perform with company members for the "Nutcracker"
  - Performances have been featured by Dance Spirit Magazine, The Atlanta Journal-Constitution, Atlanta Chinese News, and World Journal (9-12)

- Chorus (8 years)
  Georgia All-State Chorus (9-10)
  Northview Chamber Chorus (10-12)
  Northview Advanced Women's Chorus (9-10)

- Piano (11 years)
  Northview Piano Club: President (11-12)
  GMTA (Music Teacher's Association of Georgia)
  State Piano Competition:
  Master Class Winner (10 & 12)
  Outstanding Performer Winner (9-11)
  Received National Guild of Piano Teachers
  Audition – High School Diploma (12)

Clubs and Leadership

- History Club: Founder, President (11-12)
- Piano Club: President (11-12)
- Northview Beta Club (9-12): Project Manager (12), Treasurer (10-11)
- Kaleidoscope Peer Diversity and Mediation Program (10-12): Senior Officer (12)
- National Honor Society (12)
- National Spanish Honor Society (11-12)
- Tri-M Music Honor Society (10-12)
- Science Olympiad Team (11-12)
- Student Council Representative (9-10)

Community Service/Volunteer Activities

- Emory Crawford Long Hospital, Volunteer, Summer 2005 (11): volunteered in hospital's pharmacy, nursing floor, and human resource office
- National Beta Club -Northview Chapter (9-12)
  - Project Manager (12)
    Initiated and organized Southeast Asian Tsunami Fundraiser at Party City store. Money raised was donated to the American Red Cross (10)
    Created and organized the "Holiday Gift Baskets" service program for Ivy Hall Assisted Living which became an annual tradition (10-12)
  - Treasurer (10-12)
  - Received Northview VIP Award 2 consecutive years for outstanding community service contribution
- Northeast Spruill Oaks Library, Volunteer (9-10)

Work Experience

Atlanta Chinese Bilingual Arts Center –
Dance Teacher, Summer 2005 (11)

Honors/Awards

- TASP (Telluride Association Summer Program) (12)
- National AP Scholar with Distinction (12)
- National Merit Scholarship Winner (12)
- 1st Place – State Science Fair (57th Georgia Science and Engineering Fair) (10)
- IDC (International Dance Challenge) National Finals
  Art Stone Global Entertainer Award (10)
  National Senior Champion 1st Runner-Up (10)
- Georgia Certificate of Merit (11)
- Exemplar Short Story Award – Georgia Scholastic Press Association (11)
- 1st Place regional, 3rd Place state – Science Olympiad Competition (11)
- 2nd Place – Monte Jade Young Achievers Award Southeastern U.S. (11)
- Northview Outstanding TAG (Talented & Gifted) Student (1 per grade) (11)
- Northview Outstanding Science Student (12)
- Northview VIP Award (10, 11, 12)

Others: Loves to choreograph dance pieces, travel, and cook.

Essay

Dancing through Life

Curtains glide open.

It is time to dance. My heart quivers as I gaze out into the gaping vastness of the theater. The audience, that dark, excitable sea, is swiftly quelled in a torrent of suspense-filled silence. The veil concealing the stage from the audience has vanished, blurring the line between truth and fiction.

Music adds to the surrealism. Sometimes it sparkles its way in with all the sweetness and subtlety of a summer rain drizzle. Other times, it thunders in, threatening to escape the confines of the theater. The music reminds me to never miss a beat, to exalt this moment.

The feeling on stage is a glorious one. In this world of creative and infinite possibilities, I am wholly in control of my medium. Here, spontaneity of feeling emanates from outstretched limbs, open eyes, and a vivid visualization. Here, I conjure up emotions, and the audience magnifies them. Words and thoughts from the outside world are abandoned in midair as creativity casts a spell upon reality. On stage, I become a figment of the audience's imagination.

I am stunned by how powerfully dancing can stimulate the imagination and how dynamically dancing can express emotions. Dance is raw magic. Somehow, through that intangible feeling that is shared between me and my audience, something more concrete is generated - understanding. Dance truly is a universal language that lets people of different cultures better understand one another. Each time I perform a Chinese folk dance at a cultural exchange or diversity celebration event, I am moved by the applause of people from all over the world. They are not just applauding for the dance; they are applauding for Chinese culture, for a piece of the mosaic that is the world. At the same time, they inspire me to follow their example, to appreciate and applaud other cultures as well.

Dancing has exposed me to the world's cultures in beautiful ways, and I have come to appreciate the vastness and depth of human experiences. Each dance is distinctive, standing out because of the costume, the music, the movements, or sometimes just a subtle yet unforgettable flicker in the eyes. Each dance expresses the history and the worldview of its culture. I have gained through dance a deeper understanding of people around the world and the confidence to venture out into this world as a leader.

Dancing is something for which I get excited, and it is something of which I am tremendously proud. Dancing is my ticket to a world beyond reality yet still within my reach. And dancing is my expressive language that speaks insistently to the soul of each being.

After the final applause, the curtains close, and I cease to be part of the world crafted by imagination. But that imaginary world remains a part of me and of my audience. I always leave the stage with a flutter in my heart.

Jensen Law

From North Hollywood to Brown

High School

North Hollywood Highly
Gifted Magnet
5231 Colfax Avenue
North Hollywood,
CA 91601

Population of Graduating
Class: 626

Students to Ivy
League Colleges that Year: 10

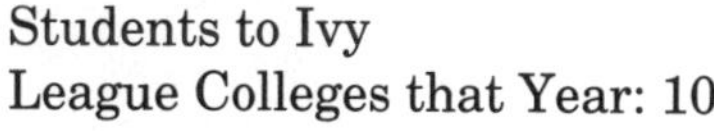

Extra-curricular Activities During High School

Sports

- Citywide Aquatics (9-12)
- Cleveland Pool summer swim team (9-12)
- 1st place breaststroke in the San Fernando Valley (11)
- 2nd place backstroke in the San Fernando Valley (11)

Music

- Played piano for 8 years
- Played violin for 5 years
- North Hollywood Orchestra (9)

Publications

- The Annual (School yearbook)
  Photographer (9-10)
  Section Editor (11)
  Editor in Chief (12)

Community Service/Volunteer

- Interact Club (Community service organization, 9-12)
  Wheels for Humanity Chairperson (10)
  Vice President (11)
- Shriners' Hospital for Children (10-12)
  Volunteer: performing magic shows for the patients and assisting in the Nursing Station
- Democratic Political Office, Volunteer (10)
- Student Poll-Worker (12)
  November 2, 2004 Presidential Election
- Hollywood Education and Literacy Project (12)
  Tutor: teaching English and reading

Leadership/Clubs

- Science Bowl (9-12)
  Captain (12)
  5th place in the United States (11)
  2nd place in Los Angeles (12)
- Science Olympiad (9-12)
  1st place in Los Angeles (10-12)
  4th place in California (10)
- Physics Bowl (11)
  Highest scoring division 1 school
- Chemistry Olympiad (11)
- Math Club (9-12)
  Participated in the American Mathematics Competition 10 & 12, qualifying to take the American Invitational Mathematics Examination (9-12)
  Bay Math League (2nd place team, 3rd place individual) (10-12)
  Math Day at the Beach (1st place) (12)
- Ultimate Frisbee Club (9-12)
- Bridge Club (10-12)
- Cricket Club (11-12)
- Boy Scouts of America (9-12)
  Eagle Scout w/ gold palm (9)
  Den Chief (9)
  Patrol Leader (11)
  Junior Assistant Scoutmaster (10-11)

Work Experience

- Private tutor
  - Chemistry (11-12)
  - Mathematics (9-12)
- Lim's Educational Center (12)
  Teaching SAT prep classes

Honors/Awards

- AP Scholar with Distinction (10)
- National AP Scholar (11)
- National Merit Scholar (12)

Others

California Scholarship Federation (9-12)
Regional Conference volunteer (10)
Seal bearer (12)

Essay

From Magician to Physician

I have been interested in the human body ever since first grade, though I was not considering a career in medicine at that age. I was curious to know how the various organs work, and I enjoyed learning about them and making various models and diagrams. I put together a representation of the lungs and diaphragm using balloons, straws, and a plastic soda bottle and demonstrated to my first-grade class how the downward contraction of the diaphragm causes the lungs to expand, allowing air to flow in.

I started considering a career in medicine when I began volunteer work at the Shriners Hospital for Children, though I was only a junior magician at first, performing magic shows for the patients. When I saw the children and learned about the hospital's mission to "provide the highest quality care to children with neuromusculoskeletal conditions, burn injuries and certain other special health care needs" at no cost to the patient or family, I became intrigued. I wanted to have a part in changing these children's lives for the better. I wanted to become a doctor.

When I became old enough, I began to volunteer as the East Nursing Unit aide so I could get a first-hand look at what it is like to work in a hospital. While I was organizing paperwork and answering the phone, I watched the doctors and nurses interact with the patients. Many patients came and went, but some stayed for over a week. I could see them slowly make their recovery and become fully functional with a skin graft or a new prosthetic limb. This strengthened my desire to go into medicine and help people.

My interest in becoming a physician was further reinforced when I joined the North Hollywood Science Bowl team. Upon joining the team, I began to study biology even before taking the class. In learning the various hormones and glands of the endocrine system, I became even more fascinated in the human body. It intrigued me that a deficiency or excess of a single molecule could lead to such disorders as diabetes and cretinism.

As a future physician, I vow to follow the ideals of the profession as stated in the PLME's Physician's Oath and Lasagna's version of the Hippocratic Oath. I will "dedicate my life to the care of the sick, the promotion of health and the service of humanity," remembering that "I do not treat a fever chart [or] a cancerous growth, but a sick human being, whose illness may affect the person's family and economic stability." Being a doctor is an honor and a privilege, as well as a great responsibility, and I will endeavor to live up to the expectations of the ideal physician.

Jason Siu Cheong Ma

From Hong Kong to Brown

High School

Li Po Chun United World College of Hong Kong (Grade 11-12)
La Salle College (Grade 9-10)

Population of Graduating Class: 124

Extra-curricular Activities During High School

Sports

- Basketball Team (11-12)
- Volleyball Team (11-12)
- Handball Team (9 -11)
- Swim Team (11-12)

Music/Arts

- Jazz Band Drummer (11-12)
- Chinese Percussion (12)

Travel

- China: Li Jiang, Xi An
  Backpacked and hiked the Tiger Leaping Gorge (11)
- Puerto Galara, Philippines
  Completed scuba diving training program specially designed for volunteers of the Hong Kong marine park (11)

- Wattala, Sri Lanka
  Volunteered for a week at the Prithipura Community, an orphanage for the mentally and physically challenged Sri Lankans (12)

Leadership

- Chinese Cultural Evening Organizing Committee, Vice Chairperson (11)
- Sport Team Captain (Basketball and Volleyball) (11)
- Challenge Day Organizer
  Led a student team to hold a range of discussions and outdoor activities to evaluate fit of the incoming class of Li Po Chun United World College (12)
- Hong Kong Union For Young Leaders
  Selected as one of two students to present La Salle College in the year long Leadership Summit; discussed and practiced leadership at simulation debates and volunteering opportunities with over 80 selected candidates from other prestigious schools (9)

Community Service/Volunteer Activities

- Coral Monitoring Team diver
  Dived regularly at the Hong Kong Marine Park, performed underwater surveys for the World Wide Fund to monitor Hong Kong's water quality (11-12)

Clubs

- Dragon Dance Team (11-12)
- International Current Affairs (A group that presents current affairs to students, and facilitates discussions on the presented topics) (11)

Work Experience

- Hong Kong and Shanghai Banking Corporation
  Personal Financial Service Summer Program (11)

Essay

Discovering my Cultural Roots-and Myself

Warm sunlight shining directly onto my face, I looked directly at the mid-day sun and closed my eyes. Standing on the third-floor balcony in LaSalle College, I felt incredibly lonely. It was not that schoolmates were unfriendly or teachers were unapproachable, but I simply had this inexplicable feeling like a pent-up lion locked inside a cage, totally neglected. I longed to break free.

Although full of ideas and enthusiasm to help bringing changes to improve the College, I was not accepted as a forward-thinking student leader, but a rebel. While I appreciated the eleven years La Salle had developed me to be the educated and caring person I was today, it was sad to admit that the pervasive old doctrines from Chinese culture had stopped the school from accepting new ideas and creativity. I knew the longer I stayed in La Salle College, the weaker the flame and passion would burn in my heart. So I took the risk to change my life and walked out of the school, unnoticed by anyone. I headed with confidence to another high school, Li Po Chun United World College (LPCUWC), hoping to grow under an education system filled with Western openness instead of Chinese conservatism.

****

It was dark upstage and the backstage was bustling with chatters about problems occurred during the rehearsal for the Chinese Cultural Evening. I picked up the walkie-talkie and requested the lighting crew to review scene five. In response, the lights came back on illuminating the once unadorned academic block, now decorated with deep red banners that fluttered in the breeze. The stage manager and program director handed me the final program list to sign off, and as the vice-chairman of the Chinese Cultural Evening Organizing Committee, I went through the run-down carefully, endorsed it and called for another full rehearsal.

I stood onstage watching as the actors prepared their parts and technicians meticulously checked the sound system for another smooth run. I felt joy and pride. Once so neglected, I was finally recognized for my talents and ideas. This College welcomed me by providing me chances to be involved in the school community and by listening to my ideas in various cultural issue discussions. Our school fosters the spirit of a strong, supportive community. Everyone in LPCUWC is treated as unique individuals who may hold drastically different viewpoints, but is also encouraged to always keep an open mind to diverse opinions. I was so thankful for the respect from my colleagues, for I didn't feel lonely anymore.

The Chinese Cultural Evening gala was originally intended to introduce our culture to the exchange students body, but its effects were far stronger than this definition: it also helped me realize how Chinese culture is surprisingly abound with engaging, aesthetic and creative art forms. I was so thrilled to learn how popular Chinese cultural performances were among my fellow schoolmates, and their talents made the show even more colorful and meaningful. The more I learned and understood the Chinese culture I once scorned, the more I loved and respected it. Now I knew it was not any Chinese doctrines that influenced my former school's attitude towards new ideas, rather, it was a system and mentality that resisted changes as if all changes would bring out undesirable results.

A final rehearsal call from the backstage cued me to the part I was responsible for. I immediately gathered myself from my thoughts and walked towards the black curtains. Behind the curtains, actresses dressed in *Qipao* (traditional Chinese gown with mandarin collar) were walking down the corridor, the stage crew were having their final meeting, and my fellow lion dance teammates were waiting for me with the costume, props and the drums. I grabbed the ornately decorated "lion head" whose wild eyes beam with joy and courage. I practiced my lion dance steps: one step, two steps. Hoisting the lion head prop from inside, I was at once a lion. Freed from any restriction, "I", the lion, danced around with proud steps and even winked by flapping the lion's eyelid from inside the prop. I jumped and jolted the head, bent and knelt down to roll.

****

The drummer stepped up the rhythm as amber stage light shone and reflected on the golden lion body. I perspired dancing and moving around inside the lion head. Rapid drum patterns prompted me to move even quicker to bring out an excited and exuberant lion. At the last loud drum beat, I leapt into the air while holding up the lion head prop above my head. I caught a glimpse of the audience. My friends, teachers, relatives and my future were all there watching in anticipation for the final dramatic leap. Suddenly waves of applause filled the auditorium at this concluding act during our final rehearsal. I knew then that I have not only found my place in the world and my roots in the process, but more importantly, I have also leapt into a new chapter of my life.

SECTION II **COLUMBIA UNIVERSITY**

Official Name:	Columbia University in the City of New York
Location:	New York, NY 10027 USA
Website:	http://www.columbia.edu
Year established:	1754 (as King's College)
Founder:	King George II of England
Motto:	*In lumine Tuo videbimus lumen* ("In Thy light shall we see light")
Mascot:	Roar-ee the Lion
Colors:	Light blue and white
Nickname:	Columbia

Undergraduate student population:	7,548 (2008-2009)
Freshmen population:	1,341 (Fall, 2008)
Domestic students	83%
International students	17%

Colleges on campus:

Columbia College
School of Engineering and Applied Science
School of General Studies
School of Nursing

Section editor: Hung-Bing Tan

Shirley Chen

From Thomas Jefferson to Columbia

High School

Thomas Jefferson High School for Science and Technology
6560 Braddock Rd.
Alexandria, VA 22312

Population of Graduating Class: 400

Students to Ivy League Colleges that Year: 30

Extra-curricular Activities During High School

Sports

- Rhythmic gymnastics (9-10)
  Region 5 Zone 3 Rhythmic Gymnastics Championships 1st Place (9-10)
  US Eastern Rhythmic Gymnastics National Championships 22nd Place (9-10)
- Ballet, jazz, lyrical dance, TJ Dance Team (9-12)
  George Mason Dance Invitational Senior Individual 1st Place (12)

Music/Arts

- Piano (9-12)

Publications

- Yearbook, school newspaper (9-12)
- Published Research Paper: "Molecular Detection of *Rickettsia ambloymmii* in *Amblyomma americanum*

Parasitizing Humans" in American Society for Rickettsiology (12)

Leadership

- Varsity Dance Team Captain (12)
- President of Hope Chinese Students Association (11)
- Director and Coordinator of Anti-Drug Performance Group - Rock Challenge (11)
- Public Relations Representative for Girls in Engineering Math and Science - GEMS (11)
- Choreographer of International Night for Chinese Culture Club (11-12)

Community Service/Volunteer Activities

- Habitat for Humanity (9-12)
- China Charity Fund: worked with CCF Chairman Malina Yung in cooperation with the NBA and Kraft Foods Co. to generate over $1 million worth of charity donations for rebuilding homes and schools in rural China (11)

Work Experience

- SAT Tutor (11-12)
- Mentorship at Walter Reed Navy Medical Research Center: Individually developed a quantitative real-time polymerase chain reaction assay for the detection of *Rickettsia ambloyommii* that demonstrates high specificity and sensitivity (12)
- Summer Research Intern at Eco-Environmental Institute of China: developed an biochemical assay for instantaneous soil pollution analysis (11)

Honors/Awards

- National Merit Scholarship Finalist (12)
- National AP Scholar (12)
- Academic Achievement Letter (9-12)

Essay

Olga

With its dramatic vaulted ceiling and sweeping ballet bars, the gym seemed dauntingly magnificent when I was twelve. For all its notable attributes, the gym was most remarkable because it was there, amidst the mania of my first rhythmic gymnastics competition, that I spotted her. Even from a distance, she was utterly captivating, with luxurious red hair and luminous honey eyes. Her body was graceful, but moved with a startling aggression - every gesture, every movement, resonating with elegant precision. I spied on her with a guilty sense of disproportionality - I was a failed gymnast, one that had started too old to ever be any good. Yet, with an anxious desperation, I hoped she would look my way.

One sharp breathe later, she was next to me, staring intensely while my muscles flexed taut and shook with unsteadiness as I demonstrated a side inclination balance. “My name is Olga. I will coach you - if you wish”.

There was no hesitation on my behalf, but my parents did not share my visions of glory. They had enrolled me in gymnastics because I was bored, not to pursue any lofty ambitions. So, I sold my soul to my parents - straight A’s and piano lessons became prerequisites for gymnastics. The fact that I could barely speak English and abhorred piano seemed to matter little at the time.

Olga never cared that I had to drive two hours per day, three days a week to train at her gym in Maryland. She didn’t care that I had to compete with girls who practiced religiously six days a week. Olga did not insult me by pitying my circumstances, instead, she taught me to overcome the limitations of my reality. Rhythmic gymnastics became the source of my hopes and dreams, my fears and my madness.

My most poignant memory of Olga was when she was sick three days before Junior Olympics. Inhaling cough medicine and positively shaking with fever, she still came to coach me. Some days I hated her – with an unrelenting severity, she confronted my sincere effort with her inevitable criticism, and opted to push me harder when I was already trying my hardest. She coached with a dramatic urgency that made everything but the practice at hand seem superfluous. Olga drove me beyond my breaking point and showed me that talent without hard work was worthless.

Once, in a burst of epiphany, I realized *this* was love. Even when she was sick and unappreciated, Olga came because she was needed. Her resilience challenged me to face life with an equivalent tenacity. Somehow, this short frail Russian woman turned a shy twelve-year-old girl into a fierce competitor, both at the gym and in life.

Olga is family - we share an inexplicable emotional bond forged by our reciprocal faith in each other. She gave me ambition, taught me graciousness, and inspires me daily with her actions and words. I kept that promise I made to my parents so many years ago, more for myself than anyone else now. Piano became a venue to release my inner angst, while my competitiveness and delight in learning endeared me to academics. No matter what I do in life, I know that the passion with which I pursue any of my dreams stems from a woman named Olga Irina Kutuzova.

Mendi Sui

From San Mateo to Columbia

High School

San Mateo High School
506 N. Delaware St.
San Mateo, CA 94401

Population of Graduating Class: 350

Students to Ivy League Colleges that Year: 3

Extra-curricular Activities During High School

Sports

- Cross Country (10-12)
  Varsity all 3 years, Team Captain (12), Sophomore Athlete of the Year Award (10), Most Valuable Athlete Award (11), Central Coast Section Participant (11-12),
- Track & Field (9-11)
  Varsity 2 years, Peninsula Athletic League Champion (in 1600 meters) (10), All-League Athlete (10), Central Coast Section Participant (11)

Music/Arts

- Piano (9-10)
  Certificate of Merit Tests (up to Level 9)
- Violin (9-12)
  El Camino Youth Symphony (9-12): Co-Assistant Concertmistress for Preparatory Orchestra (9)

- Viola (11-12)
  El Camino Youth Symphony: Assistant Principal for Viola Section of Premier Symphony Orchestra (12)

Travel

- Taiwan and Japan, tour around countries (9-12)
- England, Finland, Estonia, Russia (11)
  Tour with El Camino Youth Symphony (performed in various venues around Europe)

Community Service/Volunteer Activities

- Foster City Library Volunteer (9)
  Helped the library organize shelves and books and performed other tasks within the library.
- Homework Central Tutor (10-11)
  Worked with/Tutored students at a local church.
- Student-Organized String Quartet (11-12)
  Performed at Stanford Cancer Center: Played in a quartet (Violin) for patients and staff of the Cancer Center to enjoy.

  Performed at San Jose City Hall Rotunda: Provided background reception music for an annual non-profit Gala.
- Buddhist Temple Youth Group (11-12)
- Community Service at Golden Gate Park (San Francisco): Cleaned up the park by weeding, planting flowers, planting trees.

Honors/Awards

- California Scholarship Federation Lifetime Member (for academic excellence) (9-12)
- Scholar of the Year (10-11)
  Exemplary academic excellence (highest GPA) among all Fall Sports Athletes
- AP Scholar with Distinction (11-12)
- Wellesley College Book Award (11)
  Academic excellence and leadership in the school and community
- Bank of America Achievement Award (12)
  For academic excellence

Essay

Crossing the "Border"

I accredited *everything* to being Asian: my hard work, my ambition, my talents. Instead of the Gatsbian "American dream," I deemed my desires for success the "*Asian*-American dream" - to work *twice* as hard and become successful - just like my forefathers had. Attempting to mask my pride, I lived my life as a modest, obedient girl - unsuccessfully so, for I was furtively draping myself under a "little Asian girl" cloak. "Little Asian girls never got into trouble and could always be trusted," I told myself, fueling my ethnocentric beliefs. Deep down, I knew my ideas were flawed, and a series of events this past summer would alter them thereafter.

Last summer, I traveled to Finland, Estonia, and Russia with the El Camino Youth Symphony. Our orchestra was predominantly Asian, a factor I have always considered a great contributor to our success. In Europe, I hoped to establish a positive Asian-American presence, but I was overzealous: like Napoleon traversing Europe in efforts to glorify France, I hoped to do my part for the *Asian* race - just on a smaller scale. Upon arriving, I was disappointed. I expected the Europeans to accredit our successes as an orchestra to our widely Asian constituency. Instead, the enraptured audiences merely commended the "professionalism" and "youthfulness" of our group. *What's wrong with these people?* I questioned. On the train crossing the Russian border, I discovered my answer: *Nothing*.

Sitting nervously as the train came to a halt, I anticipated a smooth border-crossing - after all, we were all kind-hearted, respectful Asians. As the border-patrol officers stepped aboard the train, I felt my nerves tighten. *They couldn't really be paranoid over a train of Asians, right?* They meticulously search my cabin, and I greeted them with my "little Asian girl" politeness, hoping they would notice. To my dismay, their strict demeanor did not alter. They proceeded in the same manner, as if I hadn't even courteously attempted a Russian "hello" or "thank you." It was at that very moment, when, in the very place Napoleon met *his* defeat, I discovered the pitfalls of my own beliefs. It became clear to me: the guards didn't care if I was Asian - we were under the same scrutiny as anyone who would cross the Russian border, whether a criminal or a saint. In any case, being Asian didn't *mean* anything in terms of character or personality - it's the individual. While I scoffed at the absurdity of other stereotypes - African-Americans are good at basketball, Latinos are good at soccer - I was creating my own, but on what grounds? Absolutely none. The meaningless label called "Asian", in my case, did *not* necessarily equate to being "intelligent" or "gifted". My ethnocentric beliefs were tenuous: I was obviously mistaken to pride my talents simply on my race. After all, I wasn't a puppet, and the label "Asian", a ruthless puppeteer controlling my various thoughts and actions. Likewise, the fact that my orchestra is ninety-nine percent Asian had nothing to do with our successes; renowned author Amy Tan isn't an exceptional writer because she is Asian, but because she possesses an undeniable literary talent. Talent does *not* root from ethnicity.

As I spanned the courtyard the first day of my senior year this fall, only to find the same cliques and groups as the year before, I suddenly realized that no longer was the Asian crowd - my crowd - the only "smart and talented group" in the school: students not only of different races, but of different religions and socioeconomic backgrounds constantly excel in and out of the world of academia - like that African-American boy who has helped me with my English homework on many occasions, and that Caucasian girl who takes five AP classes and still manages to work two jobs. Race has become irrelevant.

Through this, I now view my accomplishments as *surpassing* the insignificant label of ethnicity: my accomplishments are representative of *my own* person. As I stop and reflect on all that had occurred just this past summer, I realize that, in the course of these events, my nationality had not changed, but I had.

Hung-Bing Tan

From Enloe to Columbia

High School

William G. Enloe High School
128 Clarendon Crescent
Raleigh, North Carolina
27610

Population of Graduating Class: 488

Students to Ivy League Colleges that Year: 4

Extra-curricular Activities During High School

Sports

- Soccer (9-12)
- Rugby (12)

Music/Arts

- Piano: 10 years and participated in annual competitions (9-12)

Leadership

- Science Olympiad: Co-President (11-12)
- Triangle Area Chinese American Society Youth Group (Vice-President, 11; President, 12)
- Triangle Area Chinese American Society Youth Symphony (Vice-President, 11)
- Economics Club (Vice-President, 12)
- Future Problem Solving Team (Board member, 10-11)

Community Service/Volunteer Activities

- WakeMed Hospital Junior Volunteer (11-12)

- Member of Key Club International (10-11)

Clubs

- Science Olympiad (9-12)
- Economics Club (11-12)
- National Honor Society (12)
- American Computer Science League (9-12)
- Triangle Area Chinese American Society Youth Group (9-12)
- Future Problem Solving Team (9-11)
- Speech and Debate (10)

Work Experience

- Summer Research Intern at Duke University studying carbon nanotubes (11-12)
- Meat/Seafood Clerk at Whole Foods (12)

Honors/Awards

- National Merit Scholarship Finalist (12)
- National AP Scholar (10-12)
- Siemens Competition Regional Finalist (12)
- North Carolina State Science Fair 1st Place Team (12)
- American Computer Science League Southern Division 1st Place (11)
- Intel Science and Engineering Fair 3rd Place Grand Award (12)
- North Carolina NCEE Economics Challenge 1st Place (11)

Essay

Believing in Democracy

"Most people here today are underclassmen... What if our guy doesn't win..."

"Don't worry, that freshman won't win. And if he does, we'll just follow precedent."

"I guess...let's begin," I responded as somewhat worriedly I started the election.

Enloe's Science Olympiad club ended the 2005-2006 year on a high. During my first year as a co-President, the team's performance increased from 10th place to 3rd place at the state competition. The club's future seemed very promising until, in the final act of the 2005-2006 year, we held elections.

The Science Olympiad club at my high school has never strictly held themselves to democratic standards. Despite the existence of an election, both precedence and the club's constitution (which had become progressively ambiguous over the last few years) grant the current board full discretion in selecting the next year's board members. However, as we tallied up the election results, I could see ten-fold the same feelings of uneasiness that I had entering the election.

One member of the current board was graduating and the remaining three of us automatically retained our positions. Prior to the election, we already had an ideal replacement in mind, honestly thinking that our favorite was clearly the best candidate to the entire team. However, Justin, a freshman who had shown questionable maturity by being disruptive during meetings and competitions, seemed to have a lot of underclassmen support. Justin won by a single vote. I was worried that he would not be constructive as a board member and would interfere with my senior year goal of leading the team to the national competition.

The other board members suggested that we consider exercising our constitutional powers, but I couldn't come to terms with that decision, especially since I was initially denied a spot on the board after a previous election despite winning a true majority. We eventually decided to simply sit down and talk with Justin. To my astonishment, he agreed with our concerns regarding his leadership ability and recognized his own inexperience and immaturity. Even more reassuring were his reasons for running for a position: to learn and gain experience to help the club when the remainder of the current board graduates the next year. We decided to place our faith in the democratic process as our conversation moved towards the responsibilities of our newest board member.

It did not matter that the votes were so close, that we had our doubts, or that making our own decision was constitutional – he had earned it. In the past, board members believed the act of leading included handpicking future leaders of our club regardless of group consensus. However, I felt that integrity, fairness, and trust are also important leadership qualities to provide. Despite our concerns, a large portion of the club showed confidence in Justin and we decided to place our faith in the wisdom of our teammates. Who was I to overrule any decision that the club collectively decided? This conflict taught me that it's important to have faith in the wisdom of others, a faith that I have since tried to maintain whenever working with groups or teams.

SECTION III **CORNELL UNIVERSITY**

Official Name:	Cornell University
Location:	Ithaca, NY 14853 USA
Other campuses:	New York City, NY Education City, Qatar
Website:	http://www.cornell.edu
Year established:	1865
Founders:	Ezra Cornell Andrew Dickson White
Motto:	"I would found an institution where any person can find instruction in any study"
Mascot:	The unofficial mascot is the bear
Colors:	Carnelian and white
Nickname:	Big Red

Undergraduate student population:	13,846 (Fall, 2008)
Freshmen population:	3,139 (2008)
Domestic students:	91%
International students:	9%

Colleges on campus:

College of Agriculture and Life Sciences
College of Architecture, Art, and Planning
College of Arts and Sciences
College of Engineering
School of Hotel Administration
College of Human Ecology
School of Industrial and Labor Relations

Section editor: Robert W. Fu

Robert W. Fu

From Paideia to Cornell

High School

Paideia School
1509 Ponce De Leon Ave
Atlanta, Georgia 30307

Population of Graduating Class: 96

Students to Ivy League Colleges that Year: 6

Extra-curricular Activities During High School

Sports

- Varsity Cross Country (10-12)
  Most Improved Runner (10)
  Coach's Award (11)
  Career Achievement Award (12)
- School Tennis Team (9-11)

Music/Arts

- Piano
- Violin
- Guitar

Leadership

- Science Olympiad , Captain (11-12)
- Varsity Cross Country, Co-Captain (11)
- Anime Club, Co-President (11-12)

Community Service/Volunteer Activities

- Volunteer at Frazer Center (12)

Worked as an assistant in a classroom with 5-7 year old children, some mentally underdeveloped

- School Fundraising
  Volunteered in school auction. Creatively presented items during auction and served during the auction dinner.
- Website Building for
  Cross Country Team
  Robotics Team
  Paideia School's Student Newsletter

Clubs

- Science Olympiad (4-12)
  Awards: Receive various medals from regional and state competition each year.
  Leadership: Captain (11-12)
- Robotics Team (11-12)
  Web and Graphics designer, Robot builder
- Academic Bowl (9-12)
  Second place at region (9)
  Second place at region (10)
- Anime Club (12)
- Math Team (10)
- 3-D Modeling Projects (7-10)
  3-D modeled for some online projects that involved modifying computer games and making new ones

Mentoring/Teaching Experience

- Mentorship for junior high students (11)
- Computer Class (12)
  Taught a course at Paideia high school on computer hardware. Raised fund to build a PC for the class. The computer was donated to the school.

Work Experience

- Summer of 2003, Biomedical laboratory research (volunteer), Emory University
- Summer of 2004, Laboratory automation assistant, Emory University

- Summer of 2005, Winship Cancer Institute internship; Joined the Lung Cancer Program Project team as Web designer and database builder

Publications

- The New Age of Piracy *The Forum*, Nov. 2003
- Land Yourself at a LAN party *The Forum*, Dec. 2003
- iPod vs All *The Forum*, Feb. 2004
- Identity Theft Increasing, Consumers Unsuspecting *The Forum*, Apr. 2004
  (*The Forum* is the Paideia School student run newspaper)

Essay

Transition Points

When you see someone on the street, their lives are just moving along and you meet them partway through a stage of their lives. However, it is seeing people at transition points in their lives that most poignantly illuminates the value of human life. While working at the Winship Cancer Institute last summer, I got a rare opportunity to follow Drs. Khuri and Funuchi into the cancer clinic. I had worked with ailing people before - with disabled children in the Frazer Center and adults in hospitals - but what I experienced in that clinic was different from any of those encounters.

Many patients who came to the clinic were at the end of a pivotal stage in their lives. Witnessing their anxiety as they tried to find out what was going to happen to them made my experience especially impactful. One patient's story was particularly disheartening. He had gone through three types of treatment for his cancer without any response. When he came in that day, he told Dr. Khuri that he had given up on treatment and was just going to live with cancer. I felt sad but deeply moved by his courage and dignity.

Another patient had just been diagnosed with cancer. She looked terrified. Would her treatment work? What would her life be like? How much longer would she live? Instantly, my image of life changed. Life is so fragile; we may not even notice it. But something like cancer could be sapping away at it and we would not be able to do much about it. We urgently need to develop more advanced technologies to dramatically improve medical testing and treatments.

A third patient came in for a tri-monthly checkup and discovered that his cancer was almost completely gone. He had been under treatment for years and had only recently experienced success. But that day he was ready to be eased off treatment; he was a cancer survivor. I felt truly happy for him and also sensed a glimmer of hope for others. His success showed that advancements in technology are worthwhile and that they really can save lives.

These three patients were defining for me – illustrating both the frailty and value of human life while at the same time reminding me of the hope and promise of modern medicine and technology to make profound differences in people's lives. Since my summer experience at Winship, I have felt a stronger sense of responsibility - urgency, really - to work on behalf of people like those I encountered there. My future goal is to use my passion, skills, and experience in computers and technology to advance medical sciences. I started the day in the clinic as a by-stander. Now, I have found human faces to help fuel my endeavors at college and beyond.

Ran Shao

From Marjory Stoneman Douglas to Cornell

High School

Marjory Stoneman Douglas
High School
5901 Pine Island Road
Parkland, FL 33076

Population of Graduating
Class: 710

Students to Ivy
League Colleges that Year:
4

Extra-curricular Activities During High School

Sports

- Cheerleading (10-12)
  Varsity Letter recipient in grades 11 and 12

Music/Arts

- Piano (7 years)
- Orchestra (11-12)
  First Chair piano, percussion
- Chinese Brush Painting (10-11)
- Color Guard, MSD Marching Eagles (9)

Leadership

- Orchestra Librarian (12)

Community Service/Volunteer Activities

- Mu Alpha Theta math tutoring in algebra, geometry, pre-calculus (10-12)

Clubs

- Mu Alpha Theta math honor society (10-12)
- Art Club (9)

Work Experience

- Private tutoring for high school students in various math subjects

Honors/Awards

- Honors Diploma (GPA 3.75+)
- Florida Bright Futures Scholar
- 1st place Martin Luther King Jr. art contest
- National AP Scholar
- Florida Marching Band Association 2006 Best Color Guard

Essay

A Melting Pot

It was easy to tell, even by the young and naïve, that I was different from my predominantly Caucasian classmates. My hair was black and stick-straight, and my eyes not only occupied a smaller portion of my face, but they sat at an awkward slanted angle. Kids often insultingly spoke fake Chinese to me or pulled at their eyes to mimic mine, all the while asking, "Why do you look like that?" I wanted nothing more than to blend in with everyone else, an obsession that occupied my thoughts from when I moved to America in elementary school until my junior year in high school. I did everything short of getting plastic surgery and changing my name to assimilate into the American culture, but I always felt that I hadn't quite gotten anywhere as my alien appearance made it impossible to blend in.

However, I remember the moment when I finally became white.

At the age of sixteen, I was given an opportunity to go back to China to visit relatives for two weeks during the summer. Upon my arrival, I was surprised to find that I felt strangely out of place: my clothes were different, my makeup was more extravagant, and my facial acne more prevalent. I felt as though everyone could tell that I am an American.

My feelings were confirmed by the observations made by my relatives. They were confused about the metal squares and wires wrapped around my teeth – very few Chinese teenagers wear braces, after all. I also apparently spoke Mandarin with an "American" accent. I used chopsticks incorrectly, complained about having to walk everywhere, and stopped at a McDonald's every chance I got. Furthermore, I had a lot of trouble communicating with everyone, whether it was my hairdresser or a cashier, and my stomach was not accustomed to the less clean water. I felt like a tourist in my own native country. Spending so much time in the United States actually had a surprisingly profound effect on me, something I didn't recognize it, and perhaps took for granted, until this experience.

When I returned to the United States, I once again became Chinese. I felt as though I were in limbo: I couldn't completely assimilate into Western culture because of my physical appearance, but I also couldn't fit in with the Chinese because of my upbringing in a different country. Rather than being frustrated, I realized that sticking out in a crowd isn't necessarily a bad thing. In fact, I can feel unique wherever I go: my trip to China opened up my squinty eyes to the cultural diversity that I embody. I no longer felt embarrassed by the rice and stir fry my mom packed for my lunch (instead of a peanut butter and jelly sandwich), or hid my Chinese pop CDs. I feel happy to be an Asian-American – a human melting pot for two different exciting cultures.

Yuan Ge

From Xi'an to Cornell

High School

High School affiliated to
Northwestern Polytechnic
University
Xi'an, Shaanxi
China

Population of Graduating
Class: 660

Students to Ivy
League Colleges that Year:
1

Extra-curricular Activities During High School

Sports

- Badminton Club, player & organizer

Music/Arts

- Piano (Level 10 Certificate, Provincial Music Education Examination Committee)
- Flute, School Orchestra

Leadership

- Chemistry Competition team (team captain, 10th grade)
- School Student Activity Committee Coordinator of extracurricular activities and physical education

Tutoring

- Private piano tutor (9th grade)
- Private English tutor

Honors/Awards

- Outstanding Student Leader (12th grade, rewarded for 5 years of work as the extracurricular activities and physical education coordinator)
- Honor Student (from 7th to 11th grade, rewarded to students with outstanding GPA and extracurricular performance)
- National Mathematics Olympiad (2004, Third Place Award)
- National Chemistry Olympiad (2004, Second Place Award)
- School Chemistry Competition (2005, Winner)

Essay

My Dream

My current dream is to cultivate myself in an innovative and energetic academic environment to prepare for a successful engineering career. This is not just my dream, but also a family dream. Eleven years ago, my father was admitted to several US graduate schools, but my family could not afford the high tuition then. Although my father tried everything he could, adding all potential incomes of part-time jobs on and off campus, the money can hardly cover the cost of living and studying. He could go, but I may have to transfer to a cheaper public school or give up my piano lessons, or my mom had to take part-time jobs after work. Finally he hid the offer and visa, his two years hard working, in a storage box. He gave up his opportunity to study in a great academic institute to guarantee a comfortable life for the family. Without his sacrifice, I may never have gotten the chance to apply the undergraduate admission to Cornell University. My father achieved success in his career years later, but he still feel sorry about his dream. Now I have grown up and realized what sacrifice my father made because I know how attractive it is to receive education in an acclaimed, multicultural academic institute like Cornell. I feel grateful that my family now has the ability to support me financially to study abroad. And I have worked hard to qualify for an education in a world-leading school. I think it is the time to make the dream come true.

Not only being the inspiration, my family has also influenced me greatly in how to realize a dream. My parents are both outstanding, self-made people. I learnt their way of working hard and pursuing what they want. Four years ago, I faced a hard situation. The national piano certificate examination conflicted with my finals. There were five long musical texts to remember and practice while I had to study hard to keep my academic performance in school. I had thought about giving up piano exam under such a stress. But this would certainly be my life-long pity if I had. It was my parents who kept encouraging me not to give up any dream and surrender to the fear and stress. They advised me to consider this a valuable challenge. I carried on, and surprisingly, found this "Mission Impossible" not as bad as it looked when I stopped imagine the hardness. This year, when I was preparing SAT and TOEFL while having to do the most rigorous Chinese school program, I benefited from the past experience of working under stress. The time consuming test preparations and applications could not scare me. I have learnt how to defeat the difficulties and to chase my dream.

Inspired and shaped by my family, I am now ready to achieve my current dream and whatever may come in the future.

SECTION IV **DARTMOUTH COLLEGE**

Official Name:	Dartmouth College
Location:	Hanover, NH 03755 USA
Website:	http://www.dartmouth.edu
Year established:	1769
Founder:	Reverend Eleazar Wheelock
Motto:	Vox clamantis in deserto "a voice crying out in the wilderness"
Mascot:	The Big Green
Colors:	Green and white
Nickname:	The Big Green

Undergraduate student population:	4,100 (2008)
Freshmen population:	1,095 (Fall 2008)
Domestic students:	92%
International students:	8%

Colleges on campus:

Dartmouth College

Section editor: Yiran Gu

Yiran Gu

From Wootton to Dartmouth

High School

Thomas S. Wootton High School
2100 Wootton Parkway
Rockville, MD 20850

Population of Graduating Class: 563

Students to Ivy League Colleges that Year: 8

Extra-curricular Activities During High School

Music/Arts

- High School Chambers Singers Choir member (9-12)
- Tri-M music honor society member and chorus representative (11-12)
- Cast member of high school musical production *Seussical the Musical* (12)
- Maryland All State Chorus (9-12)
- Montgomery County Youth Chorus (9-12)

Leadership

- Founder and Co-President of Roots and Shoots, Wootton High School chapter (11-12). Roots and Shoots is an international organization founded by the renowned primatologist, environmentalist and humanitarian Jane Goodall, aimed at inspiring youth to make real changes.

- Junior representative in Spread the Joy Club (11). Club members fundraised and delivered cards, toys, and books to children staying in local hospitals

Volunteer Activities/Community Service

- Receptionist at Rockville Library, a local public library (10-12)
- Volunteered at the Wilson Health Care Center of Asbury Methodist Village and spent weekends accompanying senior citizens with medical needs (11-12)
- Served on the volunteer jury at Teen Court, a local Justice Department program aimed to provide alternative punishments for youth caught committing minor misdemeanors (10-12)

Clubs

- Patriot Ambassadors, selective club whose members serve as representatives and student liaisons for Wootton High School (11-12)
- Envirothon team - competed in local Envirothon competitions (11)
- Spread the Joy Club (10-12)

Honors/Awards

- National Honor Society (10-12)
- French Honor Society (12)
- National AP Scholar (12)
- The Dartmouth Club Book Award (12)

Additional Information:

Grew up with grandparents in Beijing, China; moved to the U.S. from China at age 12, speaking no English.

Essay

The Power of a Smile

Have you ever felt the helplessness of a fish out of water? How about the desperation of being lost in a forest? If you had to leave behind your family and friends, your niche, and your hometown, to adapt to a new society, whose language, rules, and cultural values are dramatically different from the ones you grew up with, you would know the feeling.

And that was exactly how I felt as a twelve-year-old-girl moving from China to the United States. Although reuniting with my parents after ten years of separation was delightful, the distress I felt in this new environment overwhelmed me instantly. I did not understand the language spoken and had no way of communicating with the people around me. Even my parents were not emotionally close, since they rarely existed as much more than "mom" and "dad" written on cards and letters they had sent me from the U.S. on special occasions. I felt extremely lonely and was desperate to go back to being who I was. My only hope was that school would avert me from my constant state of misery.

To my disappointment, the first few days of school did not improve my situation. On the contrary, they heightened my despair. By the end of each day, my only desire was to go home and cry until my tears ran dry. I felt like I was lost at sea without a compass—I didn't know where I was going, what I was supposed to be doing or what the teachers and students were talking about. I had no friends to eat lunch with and nobody to talk to. I dreamed that I was back in China again, living happily with my family and friends, only to be awakened by the harsh reality that plunged me into a deeper sadness.

My days were always gloomy, until the day a friendly face appeared and brought sunshine back into my life. It was my first day in a new history class. After sitting down at the back of the room, my teacher introduced me to the class. Instead of turning back to look out of curiosity, the boy sitting in front of me smiled and extended his large, gentle hand towards me. I was so overwhelmed by this tiny act of hospitality that I almost forgot to smile back and shake his hand. But when I finally did, I felt a wave of warmth spread through my body. I didn't know that a simple smile and a firm handshake were all I needed to overcome my despair and face the challenges with determination. Every part of me felt pleasant; I sat up taller, and my breathing became more even and calm. Life was finally enjoyable again.

Ever since that day, I have tried to smile every day, reminding myself and those around me that nothing is as awful as it seems. No obstacle is impossible to overcome. All challenges become manageable when faced with a bright smile and an optimistic attitude.

Eric Hsu

From Stevens to Dartmouth

High School

John P Stevens
High School
855 Grove Ave
Edison, NJ 08820

Population of
Graduating Class: 550

Students to Ivy
League Colleges that
Year: 18

Extra-curricular Activities During High School

Sports

- Cross Country (9-10)
- Track (9-10)
- Ultimate Frisbee (9-11)

Music/Arts

- Violin
- Piano

Leadership

- Computer Club President (12)
- Law Club President (12)
- Chemistry and Physics Club Treasurer (12)

Community Service/Volunteer Activities

- Wang Da Zhong Puppet Show - a Chinese Puppet Troupe based in Middlesex County, New Jersey. The puppet troupe has performed at Rutgers University, Highland Park Elementary School, The New Jersey Chinese Festival at Liberty State Park, etc. (9-10)
- YMCA Swimming Instructor (9)

- Union Chinese School Volunteer
  Organized Chinese New Year Events (9-12)

Clubs

- Computer Club (10-12)
- Law Club (11-12)
- Chemistry Physics Club (9-12)
- Model United Nations (9-11)
- Odyssey of the Mind (9-12)
- Science League (11-12)

Mentoring or Teaching Activities

- Union Chinese School Teacher (10)
- Cambridge English Learning Center Lecturer (Taiwan) – Lectured to Taiwanese students and taught English to Chinese locals (9)

Work Experience

- SAT and AP Tutor (11-12)

Honors/Awards

- New Jersey Chinese American Cultural Association Speech Contest Champion (2004)
- NJ Governor's School of Engineering and Technology Alumni. The prestigious Governor's School only selects 100 students in NJ in 2006
- Odyssey of the Mind NJ 2nd Place and World Finalist. Competed in structure and technology competitions, placing high at states and became a World Finalist (2006)
- National Merit Corporate Scholarship Winner
- Chinese American Hai Hua Scholarship. Awarded to outstanding Chinese American students by the Association of Chinese Schools in the United States.
- Columbia University Science Honors Program Student. Passed an entrance examination and enrolled into Columbia University's Science Honors Program and studied Psychology, Astronomy, Human Physiology, and Organic Chemistry. (11-12)
- National Honors Society (11-12)
- Spanish Honors Society (11-12)
- History Honors Society (12)

Essay

The Map of My World

Preparation Step

1: Open Google maps.

2: Type in 39 Wintergreen Avenue East, Edison NJ 08820.

3. Press enter and zoom in.

If you look at the highlighted part of the Google map, you're probably looking at my house, the place where I spent the greater portion of my life – my home, sweet home. This is the starting point from which everything else began; my first robot fighting victory was won in the front yard, and it was in the backyard hole that I found my first dinosaur bone. But two years later at the age of five, when I was chased around the house by the neighbor's dog seeking its buried wishbone, I realized that the robot I was fighting was really a plum tree and that my excavated treasure came from a chicken. That was when I decided that I wanted to go play at school.

My parents were happy that I wanted to go to school and enrolled me in Christopher's Academy Preschool. But the ever little and fickle me changed my mind halfway on the car ride and when my parents dropped me off, I was a crying and wailing ball of misery. Regardless, I eventually grew accustomed to the Academy and even started attending Chinese School.

Starting at age four, I studied at Union Chinese School on Saturdays. There, as I assimilated oriental language and culture, I forged lifelong friendships and found confidence through speech contests. With the support of my parents and the Chinese School community, I delivered orations in school, county, then eastern coast region competitions. I enjoyed refining my rhetoric and approaches, and soon had the privilege of feeling the cool touch of gold within my hands.

Many years later, I found myself in high school. The public speaking experiences I carried under my belt convinced me to join the debate club in high school and create a new law club. In these intellectually stimulating environments, I debated with other students and entered mock trial competitions. I loved organizing activities, planning guest speaker sessions with the mayor and supervising fund raisers. By the end of junior year, I wanted to become a CEO and a lawyer.

Then came Governor's School of Engineering and Technology in late June. It was an extraordinary experience that changed my outlook on science. One week into the program, I relived the thrill of a boy unwrapping presents on Christmas morning when I opened a plain looking box and found a LEGO Mindstorms set inside. I was asked to construct and program several robots: an obstacle course runner and rescue vehicle, an animal, and a sumo wrestler. Tinkering with the wiring as I built my creation out of LEGOs, I also pieced together a fascination for engineering. By the end of the program, I wanted to become a CEO, lawyer, *and* an engineer.

But right now, as a senior in high school, I want to become something else. I realize that it is difficult to accomplish my dreams without a proper education. Look at the Google Map again and type in Hanover, New Hampshire. Press enter and zoom in twice. Right now, I want to become a college student at Dartmouth College.

John Li Shi

From Carmel to Dartmouth

High School

Carmel High School
520 East Main Street
Camel, IN 46032

Population of Graduating Class:
998

Students to Ivy
League Colleges that Year: 22

Extra-curricular Activities During High School

Sports

- Track and field, non-varsity (9-10)
  100m in 9th grade and 800m in 10th grade

Music/Arts

- Band, first chair clarinet (9)
- Self-taught photographer. Submitted several prints to local photojournalism contests. Won awards at Ball State University's journalism workshops for photography (10-12)

Publications

- Hilite Newspaper. Student-run newspaper at Carmel High School. Spearheaded the development of the online component, http://hilite.org (9-12).
- SLCentral.com (http://slcentral.com). Technology-review web publication, exclusively internet based. I wrote reviews here for 2 years before being promoted to Chief Editor.

Leadership

- Vice President of German Club (10-12)
- President of Amnesty International (11-12)
- Hilite News editor and news section designer (11)
- Hilite Managing Editor/Director (12)
- SLCentral.com editor (11-12)
- Project Manager at BitWise Fellows (11-12) http://bitwisefellows.com is a local company specializing in web design and development.

Volunteer Activities

- Chinese culture camp counselor (rising 10th grade summer). Translator for Chinese-speaking cultural teachers and looked after enrolled children (7-10 year old).

Clubs

- Amnesty International
- Hilite
- German Club

Work Experience

- Project manager at BitWise Fellows (11-12)
- Photographer for Carmel Clay Parks and Recreation (summers following 11-12 grade)
- Editor for online publication SLCentral.com

Honors/Awards

- First Place Ryan White Excellence in Journalism Award for Editorial and Commentary (11), for my op-ed piece on the failure of current sex education policies to curb pregnancy/disease/abortion in the state of Indiana.
- Scholar Athlete (9,10), awarded to those on an athletic team with a GPA of > 3.5
- National AP Scholar (11). Awarded to those who completed 10 AP exams with an average score of > 4
- American Association for Teachers of German 2006 Study Trip Scholarship Winner (10), AATG/PAD all-expenses paid trip to Germany awarded after application and interview process.
- National Honor Society (12)
- National Merit Finalist (12)

Essay

Enterprising Rocks

Anxious seconds tick by as the grey-haired man in the pinstripe suit touches his furrowed brow and looks thoughtfully at his notes. And though I slowly flip the pages on my legal pad as if I am calmly going over my papers, I feel a bead of perspiration forming on my forehead. This is the critical moment, the small but decisive instant in which a deal is either closed or lost. My heart beat in my ears. I gulp nervously. I am on edge, excited.

And yet, as the combination of emotional and physical impulses surge through my mind, a memory resurfaces so suddenly and vividly that I temporarily lose track of my surroundings. I am no longer the project manager of BitWise Fellows–a local web firm–prickling with anticipation at the prospect that our first client may be nanoseconds away from entrusting his organization's entire online presence to us. Instead, I am standing at the door of an old lady's home with a rock in my hand and a forced smile on my face: my first sale...

If it weren't for my parents, I probably wouldn't have ever started a business selling rocks at five years of age. But because they had always affirmed the traditional Chinese virtues of frugality and discipline, I never received any type of allowance from them, nor did they ever indulge me in a toy unless a specific occurrence, like my birthday, occasioned the rare luxury. So I was relegated the other 364 days to drool over gumball machines, sit on lifeless coin-operated ponies, and tell my friends how "dumb" and "fake" their shiny new action figures were while I secretly fancied a red Power Ranger of my own.

Then, one sizzling summer afternoon as my good friend Lee and I sat on the bank of a river hunting for 'cool-looking' stones, I came up with the brilliant idea of selling rocks. I pitched the idea to my friend, who, though skeptical at first ("Can't people just come here and get free ones?" he asked perplexedly), eventually agreed to join me in the venture. We spent the rest of that afternoon hunting for the shiniest, smoothest, most unique rocks on the riverbank, and the next day, we dragged a red Radio Flyer wagon loaded with rocks to our first unsuspecting prospect–an aged woman living at the entrance of my cul-de-sac.

Flanked by my business partner, I knocked and the old lady opened the door.

“Hi, my name is John. Um. We are wondering if you want to buy a stone for fifty cents. They are the best you can find anywhere,” I said, uncurling my fingers to reveal the rock in my hand.

She furrowed her brow and eyed us peculiarly.

“Well, I’ll have to think about that,” she said quizzically.

“Um also its buy two get one free,” I offered, forcing a toothy smile.

Ms. Barnard didn’t say anything back. I began to get nervous. Maybe she’s going to tell us we’re stupid. Maybe the stones we picked weren’t good enough. Maybe she’s mean and we’re going to get in trouble for bothering her. I felt my face turn red as I looked back down at the shiny stone in my hand. Anxious seconds ticked by as Ms. Barnard stood motionless in her doorway. My heart beat in my ears. I gulped nervously.

Suddenly, she grinned.

“You’ve got a deal. Pleasure doing business with you.”

The booming voice of the suited man rouses me from my reverie, snapping me back to reality.

“Oh!” I say hastily, rising to meet his outstretched hand. “Uh, Pleasure’s ours. On behalf of the team, we sincerely appreciate your business and look forward to working with you on this project.”

The five-year-old in me smiled.

Angela Zhang

From York to Dartmouth

High School

York High School
9300 George Washington
Memorial Highway
Yorktown, VA 23692

Population of Graduating Class: 200

Students to Ivy League Colleges that Year: 4

Extra-curricular Activities During High School

Sports

- JV Cross Country (12)

Music/Arts

- Classical Piano (ages 4-16)

Publications

- York High School French National Honor Society Newsletter ("L'Éclair") (Creator and journalist, 12)

Leadership

- President and Co-founder of International Activism Club (12)
- President of Asian Club (12)
- President of French National Honor Society (12)
- Vice-Chair of Service Committee (12)
- Publicist of Service Committee (11)
- Advisory Board to Student Council Association (12)

- Publicity Chair of National Honor Society (12)

Volunteer Activities
- Charity work for International Activism Club (12)
- Volunteered at hospital in Emergency Department and Surgical Step-down (Rising 12)
- Tutoring for Freshman Seminar (11)
- Volunteered in York and Poquoson Public Library (rising 11th and 12th grade)

Clubs
- International Activism Club (12)
- Asian Club (grade 9/10/12)
- Scholastic Bowl (9-12)
- Battle of the Brains (televised quizbowl in Southeastern Virginia) (10-12)
- Model United Nations (9-12)
- National Honor Society (12)
- French National Honor Society (11-12)
- Service Committee (11-12)
- Student Council Association (12)
- French Club (11-12)
- Mu Alpha Theta (National math honor society) (10-12)

Mentoring
- Tutoring for Freshman Seminar (11)

Work Experience
- Summer Camp Counselor for New Horizons Science and Computer Summer Camp (taught Biology and Pascal programming) (rising 12th grade)

Honors/Awards
- First place in Virginia State Science & Engineering Fair (12)
- Gold Medalist in Virginia Junior Science and Humanities Symposium (10, 12)
- Participated in National Junior Science and Humanities Symposium (10)
- Member of first place team in Scholastic Bowl (9-12)
- Outstanding Delegate (Old Dominion University High School Model United Nations) (12)

- National Merit Semifinalist (12)
- Virginia Girls State Delegate (rising 12th grade)
- AP Scholar

Additional Information

- Skipped Kindergarten and 7th grade (graduated at age 15)
- EMT-B certified in state of Virginia
- Hobbies: longboarding, glowstringing, piano, airsoft, Frisbee, sketching, Chinese dance

Essay

DNA Precipitate, Water Balloon Slingshots, and Life Lessons

"Alright. Spit."

The boy reluctantly ("Do I *have* to?") spat into a beaker, the contents of which were upended into a test tube. A dash of a strange, clear concoction of apple-scented detergent and salt. Capped, shaken, swirled (but with as few bubbles as possible). A tablespoon of ethanol.

Fifteen minutes later, we trooped back to the side table with the test tubes. "Pay attention to Angela," my fellow counselor admonished the unruly campers. I poked a pipe-cleaner shaped like a hook into one of the test tubes and stirred. Everyone huddled to see the clear filaments, fine as soap bubbles, which coalesced inside the ethanol-detergent-salt solution. Drawing the pipe-cleaner out of the solution, one could discern a very fragile, nearly-transparent white hair dangling from the hook.

"That," I said dramatically, "is your DNA."

"Whoa!"

"Cool!"

"Really?"

Though I performed the same experiment twelve times to a total of about 150 excited kids that summer, I will always relish the memory of the campers' expression when they saw their own DNA isolated into a precipitate. Although some people would not appreciate such a way to spend a summer, I have come to realize it was one of the most enriching, amazing, and fun experiences of my life. Admittedly, during the beginning of the summer, I had been feeling inadequate about my choice of what to do over the summer. While my classmates were attending all kinds of costly academic camps or SAT prep classes, I had opted instead to take the job I had long coveted even as an eight-year-old making semi-solid goo myself: a position as counselor at this science and computer summer camp. I literally had my childhood dream job, but in my ultracompetitive IB class, I still felt a bit like I had missed out on something spectacular to add to my resumé.

That attitude completely reversed by the end of July. By then I had decided that it was my brilliant classmates who missed out: biggies like inspiring children to become interested in math and science, the newfound feeling of fiscal responsibility that inevitably accompanies a first job, and the ability to teach and manage classes all by myself. But they had also missed out on the seemingly trivial perks that were just as important as the "big" benefits, like shooting giant water-balloon slingshots (to teach about trajectory and force) and being ambushed everyday by at least four adoring kids armed with warm group hugs. But most importantly, it immersed me in an environment entirely different from the intense competition at my school that so frustrated me, an environment where knowledge is appreciated not for the luster it adds to a college application, but for fun and its inherent value. This was the academic paradise I craved, even if only for elementary and middle school children. I taught my campers about cells and computer programming, but I also learned about the value of responsibility and knowledge outside of a school setting and learning to stand on my own two feet. What better way could I have spent the summer?

SECTION V **HARVARD UNIVERSITY**

Official Name:	Harvard University
Location:	Cambridge, MA
Website:	http://www.harvard.edu
Year established:	1636
Founder:	Colonial Massachusetts legislature named after John Harvard
Motto:	*Veritas* (Truth)
Mascot:	John Harvard
Color:	Crimson
Nickname:	The Crimson

Undergraduate student population:	6714 (2008-2009)
Freshmen population:	1658 (2008)
Domestic students:	88%
International students:	12%

Colleges on campus:

Harvard College

Section editor: Jimmy Li

Jun Li

From Valhalla to Harvard

High School

Valhalla High School,
300 Columbus Ave
Valhalla, NY 10595

Population of Graduating Class: 100

Students to Ivy League Colleges that Year: 1

Extra-curricular Activities During High School

Sports

- Tae Kwon Do, 1st degree black belt

Music/Arts

- Jazz Band (jazz keyboardist)
- Vocal Ensemble (alto- section leader)
- Chorus (soprano)
- Band (2nd chair clarinet)
- Played with professional musicians in pit orchestra for Valhalla Drama Society's performances of "Annie Get Your Gun" and "A Funny Thing Happened on the Way to the Forum."

Leadership

- National Honor Society-President
- Student Government (9 - 11)
- Captain, Academic Quiz Bowl Team

Community Service/Volunteer Activities

- Teacher's Assistant at Huaxia Chinese School

Clubs

- National Honor Society
- Student Government
- Valhalla Drama Society
- Valhalla International Fund
- Academic Quiz Bowl Team
- Math Club

Mentoring/Teaching Activities

- Valhalla Mentoring Program
- D.A.R.E Program Mentor
- Teacher's Assistant at Huaxia Chinese School

Work Experience

- CVS Pharmacy- Pharmacy Technician

Honors/Awards

- Valedictorian
- National Merit Scholarship Program Finalist
- Mt. Pleasant Rotary International Club Student of the Month
- High Honor Roll
- Advanced Placement (AP) Scholar
- Yale Book Award
- New York State School Music Association, Level 6, Grade of "Excellent"
- Arts Honor Society Award
- Bausch and Lomb Honorary Science Award

Others

- Attended Columbia University Science Honors Program
- Attended IBM Watson Research Program

Essay

A Physical Education

When people first meet me, they don't believe that I hold a black belt in Tae Kwon Do. Perhaps it's because I stand tall at a whopping 5'2" or because I don't seem to be the violent-punching-and-kicking type, but either way I acknowledge that I am not the female incarnation of Bruce Lee. In fact, the physical training I've received only comes second to the lifestyle transformation that Tae Kwon Do has brought to my life.

As a gawky child, I tried out for every sports team imaginable, but soon discovered I was athletically challenged and didn't delight in throwing a ball around like other kids did. True to the "nerd" stereotype, I really was the last person to be picked for kickball, and I never managed to pass the pesky New York State Physical Fitness Test at the end of each year. I longed to be able to don a sports uniform and say that I was "part of the team," but I was always too many missed balls, bruised shins, and slow laps away from this fantasy. I came home from school the day I was the only player cut from the junior varsity softball team and broke down in tears, disheartened and unable to comprehend my inadequacy.

Struggling to find an athletic niche, I walked into the Tae Kwon Do *dojang* (school) as a last resort. I remember humiliating myself in class constantly and thinking that doing a spinning hook kick looked thoroughly impossible, but this time the challenge was different—I actually enjoyed it. Slowly, I mutated from not being able to do a single pushup to running up and down four flights of stairs for half an hour straight in sparring class. I quickly realized the only path to improvement was to focus on the task and forget all other distractions, a lesson that has seeped into my everyday behavior.

Over the years, Tae Kwon Do has become an integral piece of my life; it is my sanctuary. Just two days without going to class makes me grumpy and irritable because I have grown dependent on releasing my stress and connecting with people who are really *alive.* I have befriended people like Rachel, a recent Georgetown graduate willing to give me advice on just about everything, but never failing to beat me up in class, and Master Song, my favorite instructor, a self-proclaimed comedian who constantly ridicules my name by calling me "March" or "September" or whatever month it happens to be at the time.

My black belt test was the closest I have ever come to a "profound" experience. I stopped and realized that I had actually reached my goal. After hundreds of hours of breaking boards, kicking targets, and meditating, my dream of earning a black belt had finally become a reality. I found my niche at Tae Kwon Do, and I know now that my uniform and black belt with the gold stripe does not validate that I "belong." Instead, it is my newfound strength, health, and the bonds I've forged with fellow students that affirm I am truly "part of the team." From the outside, I don't appear any different from the discontented and frustrated person I was before, but I know that Tae Kwon Do has revamped my life by fulfilling my dream and shaping me into a more resolute and confident person. Oh, and this past year, I finally managed to pass that New York State Physical Fitness Test.

Lingbo Li

From Somers to Harvard

High School

Somers High School
120 Primrose Street
Lincolndale, NY 63017

Population of Graduating Class: 230

Students to Ivy League Colleges that Year: 6

Extra-curricular Activities During High School

Sports

- Goju-Te Karate and Jim Smith Karate Travel Team; 6-12 hours of training/competitions per week. Black belt, 1st degree

Music/Arts

- Web Design: Freelance designer. Created many personal websites for herself and for others with pay, including independent label Luminal Records, jazz education program The Radio Hour, and volunteered to design websites for Student Council and Marching Band.

Publications

- The Tusker Times, High School Newspaper, Co-editor in Chief.
- Gambit Literary Magazine, Prose Editor.
- The North County News, Yorktown Pennysaver Media Group, Freelance Reporter

Leadership

- Gay Straight Alliance, Co-Founder, President
- Human Rights Club, Vice-President, Treasurer
- Color Guard (Marching Band), Guard Captain
- French Club, Treasurer
- Environmental Club, Treasurer

Community Service/Volunteer activities

- Katonah Community Center, Volunteer (sort clothes, shelve and bag food)
- St. Luke's Thrift Shop, Volunteer (sort donations, hang up clothes)

Clubs

- Human Rights Club
- Gay Straight Alliance
- French Club
- Environmental Club

Mentoring/Teaching Activities

- Chinese School, Kindergarten teaching assistant
- Private tutoring, high school and college students

Work Experience

- Subbacultcha.net (now defunct). Lingbo designed her own website to sell her handmade clothing, jewelry, and art. She specialized in designing and sewing handbags, reconstructing vintage clothing, and doing pop art reproductions.

Honors

- National Honor Society

Essay

7 Prospect Street

7 Prospect Street. It's the first home I remember. It has oily wallpaper curling away from the walls. There is mold in the tile grout, stacks of magazines that no one can bear to throw away. The fridge is faulty, a Soviet era relic, gone the way of Sputnik and Gorbachev. The winters are long, but the front yard is not conducive to snow angels.

We have one TV. I watch Power Rangers, wishing I were the Pink Power Ranger but wondering if I should be the yellow one instead since she is Asian. Secretly, I know pink is better. I lust after the action figures my classmates have.

Christmas comes. The girls talk about the elaborate dollhouses they've received. The rug we're sitting on is in primary colors with the letters of the alphabet. I pick at it. I got a plastic comb and mirror. I stop believing in Santa Claus.

My father will not let me eat the wine and communion wafer at church. He tells me that I have to read the entire Bible first. I mostly enjoy arts and crafts time when I get to cut out and color the shepherds. Around age 7, my ever logical mind decides that I don't believe in God.

There is a wall on 7 Prospect Street covered in my drawings. I'm the best artist in my first grade class and my teacher sends off my painting of a buffalo in the midst of an idyllic sunset off as a gift to a visiting author. She comments on the low quality of my crayons, and the boys on the playground comment on my old clothes. I don't really understand shame. The only time I feel it is the time my mother drives around town without cleaning the copious amounts of bird crap off the car.

I'm happy. I teach myself to sew from books and sew a miniature doll for my best friend. The most exciting gift my parents give me is a bag of unwanted clothes. I sort through it, seeing another clumsy rag doll in this white jacket, a craft project in the trim of a blouse. My room is filled with things I have made, things I am reading. As an only child, I never feel lonely. I realize I have a magical ability to create stuff, find it in the trash heap, the habited mouse traps, the chokeberry bushes outside.

Many years later, I read a vignette from The House on Mango Street. It reminds me of 7 Prospect Street. I can now point and say, "That is where I used to live," but there is still no shame. I used to be too young to know any better, now I just understand.

Jimmy Li

From Parkway to Harvard

High School

Parkway Central
High School
369 N. Woods Mill Road
Chesterfield, MO 63017

Population of Graduating Class: 350

Students to Ivy League Colleges that Year: 4

Extra-curricular Activities During High School

Sports

- Racquetball
  Second Team All-State
- Lacrosse, Varsity Team

Music/Arts

- All-Suburban Orchestra, First Violin (9-12)
- High School Symphonic Orchestra

Leadership

- High School Quizbowl Team
  Varsity Team Captain (State Champion, 11th grade)
- Racquetball, Varsity Team Captain

Community Service

- Butterfly House Volunteer
- Reading to Disadvantaged Youth in Inner-city St. Louis

Mentoring

- Private tutoring, high school and college students

Honors/Awards

- National Honors Society
- Greater St. Louis Science Fair, Division Winner (10, 11)
- Excellence in Mathematics Contest, First Place, Greater St. Louis (12)
- AP Scholar with Distinction

Others

- Goldman Sachs/NCEE Economics Challenge, National Champion Team. First won district, state, and regional competitions.
- Jeopardy! Teen Tournament Semi-finalist.

Essay

Asking Questions

When I was a young child, my parents always encouraged me to ask questions. Every time they took me to the museum or the zoo, they hoped that I would have enough curiosity to ask the tour guide why the dinosaurs became extinct or why penguins cannot fly. However, I was too shy as a child and saw no reason to risk asking the proverbial stupid question just to learn a trivial tidbit of information. Unfortunately, this practice eventually developed into a habit; when I found a topic boring or irrelevant to my daily life, I often brushed it off as insignificant. It was just easier to be ignorant.

Throughout high school, my ignorance was especially noticeable in economics. Whenever my peers and teachers discussed topics like fiscal policy, the Federal Reserve, or inflation, I would feel terribly uneducated and avoid participating in the discussion. Consequently, I was surprised when our school's economics team coach, who had heard of my success in academic quiz bowl, asked me to join the team. Since a few of my good friends were on the team, I thought competing might be fun, but I did not initially join because I sought to develop an interest in economics. However, while preparing for the competition, I discovered the practicality and underlying logic behind economics. I had wrongfully assumed that economics was an esoteric field understood only by theorists and utilized only by investors. Instead, I learned that since economics tries to find ways to best satisfy human necessities and desires, its principles are used in almost every decision making process. I deeply regretted having so stubbornly chosen to be economically illiterate when information about the field was so easily accessible and comprehensible. Fascinated by this entirely new set of facts and ideas, I eagerly read through as many introductory level books as I could before the competition.

Equipped with a strong background in fundamental economics, our team competed in the NCEE/Goldman Sachs Economics Challenge and won the district, state, and regional levels of competition. We eventually traveled to New York, where we listened to captivating speakers, toured the depths of the New York Federal Reserve Bank, and eventually won the national championship in the David Ricardo Division. Our trip to New York not only further intensified my growing curiosity in economics by providing me my first direct glimpse into the professional economics arena, but also alerted me to the abundance of activity and information that I had so completely neglected. Despite what I had previously thought, economics is a highly interesting, meaningful field that simply should not be ignored.

Our team's accomplishments in the economics competition refined my mindset towards learning. Studying economics alerted me to the dangers of ignorance, while achieving success at the national level elevated my confidence in exploring new ideas. The world features such a wondrous multitude of ideas and poses so many provoking questions that it is a tragedy to just focus on a particular area, treating topics that do not directly affect daily life as trivial or unimportant. I regret starving my curiosity as a child, for there is undeniable value in asking questions. Achieving a better understanding of the world not only advances society, but also adds great joy and meaning to my own life. I now feel a greater appreciation for the diversity of ideas available for me to enjoy. At Harvard, I hope to find new ways to fuel my pursuit of knowledge and share my continually growing curiosity with others.

Alexander Tang

From Shrewsbury to Harvard

High School

St. John's High School,
378 Main Street
Shrewsbury, MA 01545

Population of Graduating Class: 230

Students to Ivy League Colleges that Year: 4

Extra-curricular Activities During High School

Sports
- Shaolin Kempo Karate, 1st degree black belt
- Recreational Soccer

Music/Arts
- Advanced Jazz Band (First Trumpet, Guitar)
- Competed at the Berklee Jazz Festival and UNH Jazz Festival with the Saint John's Festival Band.
- Poetry published in school anthology

Leadership
- Vice-President, Student Activity Council
- Vice-President, Junior Class
- Captain, Academic Decathlon Team

Community Service/Volunteer Activities
- Patient Transporter at UMass Medical Center
- Research Internship at UMass Medical School

- Moderator of Saint John's Sponsored Junior High Math Meet
- Wrapping gifts for Pine Ridge (a Native American reservation)
- Wrapping gifts for Dismas House (a rehabilitation program for ex-convicts)

Clubs
- National Honor Society
- Student Government
- Academic Decathlon
- Varsity Math Team

Mentoring/Teaching Activities
- National Honor Society Tutor

Work Experience
- Laboratory Technician at UMass Medical School

Honors/Awards
- 2009 American Gastroenterological Association Student Research Fellowship Award
- Telegram and Gazette Outstanding Academic Achiever of Saint John's Class of 2010
- Valedictorian
- 2009 Outstanding Youth of Shrewsbury Award
- National Merit Scholarship Winner
- Harvard Book Award
- Chris Kouchakdjian Award
- Brother Alan Award for Excellence in French
- Brother Plunket Award for Excellence in Mathematics
- Headmaster's List
- Advanced Placement (AP) Scholar with Distinction
- Headmaster's Scholarship for highest score on entrance exam
- Academic Decathlon State Gold and Bronze Medalist

Others
- Conducted medical research at UMass Medical School under Dr. Gyongyi Szabo
- Co-author on two published medical articles

Essay

Vocation

It was the eyes that stayed with me. They were half-lidded, as if he did not have the strength to either fully open or close them. His pupils moved slowly and deliberately to look at me when I spoke, so unlike the quick, darting eyes of every other ten year old I had ever met, or the ten year old I had been. I could see weariness in them, and nothing else, as I could see it occupied his entire being. Everything about his demeanor and actions was tailored to expend as little energy as possible, because he had little to spare. I had difficulty looking into those eyes and remembering that I was looking at a child.

The juxtaposition of his worn eyes and his young body was mirrored in his situation. He seemed so out of place and so exaggeratedly small in the cancer ward where I met him on an otherwise typical workday at UMass as a volunteer. His wheelchair swallowed up his faint form, and everything around him directly contrasted everything about him. The beeps of the monitors, the hushed conversations of nurses, the cold and sanitary lighting. His small frame was made even smaller by the almost comically large gown he was wearing. It all underscored and highlighted the stark contrast between expectation and reality, and I could feel it with painful clarity.

As I did with every patient I met as a patient transporter, I made a few jokes in an attempt to cheer him up, but even I could see how inadequate of an attempt it was. He took his time in raising his eyes to mine, and slowly drew his lips into a tired smile. I could tell that he knew what I was trying to do, as I am sure others had done the same, but he simply could muster no more than that smile. I returned the smile feebly, and wheeled him the rest of the way back to his room in silence. I helped him get into his bed, and I bade him farewell. I still recall my initial instinct to shake his hand, as if the adult nature of his situation had transformed him into an adult. I was not sure what to do, and again that feeling of inadequacy and powerlessness swept over me. Before I could decide what to do, the boy raised his own hand to take mine, and I was shocked into returning the handshake. I wished him luck, and immediately regretted doing so. He gave me the same weary smile, and I did my best to return it. I left his small room consumed by a sense of powerlessness and regret for having done so little for this child.

The idea that children should be playing and not in the hospital has become somewhat of a cliché; however, this does not subtract in any way from the gravity of the situation. The problem is commonplace, but that does not make each individual case any less of a tragedy or any more acceptable. Children do not have the psychological or mental strength to resist disease and illness in the same fashion as adults, nor should they have to. I cannot bear the thought that any child could be harmed by a condition before they have at least a fighting chance. I have not yet been able to determine what force is responsible for placing children in such conditions. I have only been made certain that whatever this force is, it must be met with an opposite and greater force, and I that must be a part of this counteracting force.

SECTION VI **PRINCETON UNIVERSITY**

Official Name:	Princeton University
Location:	Princeton, New Jersey
Website:	http://www.princeton.edu
Year established:	1746
Founders:	Jonathan Dickinson Ebenezer Pemberton Aaron Burr Sr. John Pierson William Smith Peter Van Brugh Livingston William Peartree Smith
Motto:	*Dei sub numine viget* "Under God's power she flourishes"
Mascot:	Tiger
Colors:	Orange and black
Nickname:	Tigers

Undergraduate student population:	4,981 (2008)
Freshmen population:	1,246 (2008)
Domestic students	89%
International students	11%

Colleges on campus:
College of Arts and Sciences
Woodrow Wilson School of Public and International Affairs
School of Engineering and Applied Science
School of Architecture

Section editor: Yufei Liu

Yufei Liu

From Shrewsbury to Princeton

High School

Shrewsbury High School
64 Holden St.
Shrewsbury, MA 01545

Population of Graduating Class: 287

Students to Ivy League Colleges that Year: 2

Extra-curricular Activities During High School

Academic

- National Honor Society – President (11-12)
- Academic Decathlon – President (9-12)
- Science Club (9-10)
- Math Club (9-12)
- Asian Cultural Club (11-12)
- Member of Western Massachusetts team competing in the American Regions Math League at Pennsylvania State University (9-12)

Music/Arts

- Band – Played the trumpet (9)
- Cast member of school musical production of Jekyll and Hyde (12)
- Piano (9-12)

Volunteer Work/Community Service

- Tutor in math, science, and Spanish (9-12)
- Volunteer at soup kitchen (11)

Work/Summer Experience

- Participated in the 2003 Summer Science Program (SSP) in Ojai, CA (11)

Honors/Awards

- Presidential Scholar Semifinalist (12)
- National Merit Finalist (12)
- National AP Scholar (12)
- Superintendent's Award (12)
- Valedictorian of graduating class (12)
- Association of Teachers of Mathematics in Massachusetts (ATMIM) Achievement Award and Service Award (12)
- Bausch and Lomb Science Award (11)
- Harvard Book Prize (11)
- Worcester Telegram and Gazette Student Achiever (11)
- Prize winner in Massachusetts Mathematics Olympiad (12)
- Prize winner in Worcester County Math League (9-12)
- AstraZeneca Scholarship Winner (12)
- 1st place in Mathematics in State and Regional Academic Decathlon Competition (12)
- Finalist in Massachusetts State Geography Bee (8)
- School award for Most Outstanding Student in Mathematics (12), Social Science (10), and Physics (10, 12)
- 3 Gold Medals and 1 Bronze Medal in Massachusetts Middle School Science Olympiad State Competition (7-8)

Essay

Dear Principal Primate

The Primate School: We Teach You Discipline
Monkey Village, Mars
January 3, 2344

Dear Principal Primate,

I am writing to you about the exchange student in my class who just doesn't seem to want to cooperate. On the first day of school, I came in and was greeted by the sight of three rows of students neatly sitting in desks and looking at me attentively. Then, I saw this strange looking boy from Earth in the back of the room. He was holding a ruler threateningly over his head and trying to corrupt one of our good Martian students. He said something like this: "You know Pete, this is a great room for baseball. Baseball is one of our most popular Earth sports. You'll love it. Now, here are a few rules. For the ball to be a home run it has to be hit above the windows. Anything that hits on the windows will count as a double. OK, let's play!"

I immediately stopped the two pupils and made them take their seats. Then, as I was teaching the students about blind obedience, I was constantly interrupted by the aforementioned pupil, whose name I found out to be Yufei. He kept objecting to my key points. I told him to stop interrupting and just listen. During the rest of class, he remained silent and seemed to be deep in thought as he jotted things down into a notebook. After class, I confiscated the notebook and found a huge jumble of numbers and information about stars and hurricanes. This student is wasting his time thinking about all that scientific stuff!

After lunch, I found Yufei playing baseball once again. This time, he was holding a water bottle. He was also saying something about how best to use the water in the bottle. I didn't understand his strange jargon, but it went something like this: "Hey Pete, I think I can generate some more power if I empty out the water. That would decrease the mass of the bottle and lead to some more bat speed. You see, the kinetic energy of the bottle is equal to one-half its mass times its velocity squared. Sacrificing a little mass will help because it will allow me to swing the bottle more rapidly, and the velocity term is squared. That means more energy to the ball."

I was furious that they hadn't listened to me and warned them that any more baseball playing would result in detention. Instead of listening to me, Yufei pointed out that there was absolutely no harm that baseball could do and that he and Pete would stop playing immediately when class started. The nerve of that boy to question authority! I am the authority in the classroom! How dare he second-guess what I say!

Then, while everyone else was reading the great literary classic, "The Rule" by Seymour Chimp, Yufei read this book called "The Pleasure of Finding Things Out" by Richard Feynman. That student knew very well that books by Feynman are banned, but he deliberately disobeyed the rules. Books by freethinkers poison our minds. I think Feynman is Yufei's role model, and that would explain why Yufei's such a delinquent.

Yufei obviously cannot handle our rigid rules and expectations, and I hope you understand my request to transfer him back to Earth.

Sincerely,

Gorilla Mona

Dear Mrs. Mona,

You are correct about the exchange student Yufei. His intellectual curiosity and independent ways are wrecking our school's image. I should have been more careful with my selection of Earthlings. Hopefully he'll be accepted by one of those colleges they have in Earth. I hear that those places actually encourage freethinking, curiosity, and the quest for truth.

Yours Truly,

Paul Primate

P.S. How about we have some dinner tonight? Deimos is nice this time of year and your birthday only comes once every 687 Earth days.

Gary Li

From New Hope-Solebury to Princeton

High School

New Hope-Solebury High School
180 W. Bridge St.
New Hope, PA 18938

Population of Graduating Class: 80

Students to Ivy League Colleges that Year: 1

Extra-curricular Activities During High School

Music/Art

- School Orchestra (First-chair cellist) (9-12)
- Organized a trio (two violins and a cello) to play at two nursing homes in Doylestown (Heritage Towers and Pine Run) (11)
- Performed in a trio at Art Show at Mercer Museum in Doylestown, PA (11)
- Performed in a trio for a Christian Templars Christmas Service at the Masonic Temple in Doylestown, PA (11)
- Played with the Central Jersey Symphonic Orchestra (12)
  Adult orchestra of Central New Jersey
- Played with the Bucks County Symphony (10)
  Adult orchestra of Bucks County
- Assisted the Middle School and Elementary School Orchestras (10-12)
- Assisted a beginning cellist in her cello studies (11)

Clubs

- Yearbook Committee (Business Section Editor) (11-12)
  Helped put together the Business Section of the school yearbook

Competitions

- Speech and Debate (11-12)
  Participated in Extemporaneous Speaking portion of county-wide speech and debate league competition
- Science Olympiad (11-12)
- Mathletes (10-12)
- Reading Olympics (Captain) (9-12)
- AMC 12 and AIME Mathematics Competitions (10, 11)

Leadership

- National Honor Society (Co-chair of Gardening Committee) (10-12)
- Reading Olympics (Captain, 9-12)

Volunteer Work

- Helped with a program to increase reading awareness among elementary school kids at the New Hope Library
- Assisted with the Middle School Mathcounts Team

Sports

- Boys Varsity Tennis (11-12)
  1st Doubles Junior and Senior Year

Work/Summer Experience

- Intern at Doctor Katronic Electronics Co., LTD. in China (10)
- Employee at Subway Restaurant (11-12)

Honors /Awards

- National Merit Finalist (12)
- National AP Scholar (12)
- Cello – Played in All-County (Bucks County) (9-12), All-District (Bucks and Montgomery counties) (10-12), All-Region (Six regions in Pennsylvania) (11-12), and All-State (Pennsylvania) (11-12) Orchestra

- One of 3 cellists invited to the Pennsylvania Governor's Schools for the Arts (11)
- Certificate of Distinction in the American Mathematics Competition (AMC12) (10-11)
- 3rd place in Extemporaneous Speaking in Speech and Debate League Competition (12)
- Reading Olympics Award (9-12)

Essay

Remote Hopes

Hundreds of acres of light green, budding rice plants lay glistening in the afternoon sun. A slight breeze creates a wave that rolls into the forested mountains beyond. A small creek runs through, flowing rapidly after the recent rains. A lady kneels on the bank, washing her clothes. People line the roads selling freshly harvested vegetables and conversing. A tractor passes by, raising a cloud of dust. The chatter stops, and then resumes once the dust has settled. I am one of few tourists in Shang Li, a village in the southern part of Sichuan province in China.

Sounds of laughter and joy draw me towards a group of young teenagers playing basketball on a dirt court. I approach them, wondering how it is possible for the ball to bounce in dirt; I have my answer as I step onto the court, for it is extremely hardened by the glaring and oppressive sun. The students wave for me to join. Each has a ready smile and is eager to talk. From their talk, I realize that the old, decrepit, two-story building nearby is actually their middle school – and that they are boarding students!

They talk enthusiastically about their school life and offer to give me a tour of the campus. The ground inside the schoolhouse is dirt and full of small footprints. The scuffling sounds of my feet echo, for there is little furniture. The desks are stone, the chairs are wooden, the writing materials are chalk and chalkboard. The walls creak and the lamps sway with the breeze.

The wooden ladder leading up to the second floor is losing its battle with termites. The students scamper up with no difficulty, but it wobbles as I climb. I hit my head. The ceiling is low and the halls are narrow. The bedrooms each contain a small wooden desk, a small window, two bunk beds, and no chairs; everything is crowded into a small space. In one room, small books litter the ground. Several bags of rice lay in a corner, their meals for the week. There are no computers or televisions; they do not exist in the compound. Despite these conditions, however, the students are still able to study.

One student happily mentions that a second teacher with a high school diploma recently joined the school – there are now two teachers, one for Chinese and one for arithmetic, for about eighty students. I was puzzled why there are so few teachers. They said that most teachers do not want to work in this remote village.

I was given this tour two years ago. However, the smiles and mannerisms of the students are still fresh in my mind. If I had a year, I would like to return to that small village and join those two teachers. I could teach physics or chemistry or even English. During my stay, I asked each of the students whether they were planning on going to high school and then to college. They all responded that it would be their dream, though they clearly did not think they could. Perhaps, in a year, I can help them change that.

Tom Feng

From Mississippi to Princeton

High School

Mississippi School for Math and Science
1100 College St.,
MUW-1627
Columbus, MS 39701

Population of Graduating Class: 300

Students to Ivy League colleges that year: 7

Extra-curricular Activities During High School

Music/Arts

- Art Club (Treasurer) (9-12)
- Piano (Bach Festival, Hymn Festival, Sonatina/Sonata Festival) (9-11)

Leadership

- Student Government (11-12)
- Chess Club (President) (9-12)
- Spanish Club (Vice President) (11-12)
- Frontline Tobacco Awareness Club (Co-President) (12)
- Mississippi Mu Alpha Theta (President)

Volunteer Activities/Community Service

- Beta Service Club (9-10)
- Key Club (9-10)
- Volunteer at Nursing Home (9-10)
- Walk for Diabetes (9-10)

- Light the Night Walk for Leukemia (9-10)
- Peer tutoring (9-12)
- Mentoring middle school students (10-12)

Clubs/Hobbies

- Science Bowl (11-12)
- Quiz Bowl (9-12)
- Intramural Basketball (9-12)
- Recreational Ultimate Frisbee (9-12)

Work/Summer Experience

- Biomedical research at the University of Mississippi Medical Center (11-12)

Honors /Awards

- Presidential Freedom Scholarship (12)
- Intel International Science and Engineering Fair Finalist (12)
- Grand Prize Winner for Tylenol Scholarship (12)
- Coca-Cola Scholar (12)
- Walmart Volunteer Service Award (12)
- 2nd in Most Valuable Student, National Elks Foundation (12)
- National AP Scholar (12)
- 1st place in State Chess Competition (11-12)
- 1st place in University of Alabama Math Tournament (12)
- 1st place in School Physics Olympiad competition (12)
- 1st place in Mississippi State University Full Moon Physics Competition (12)
- 1st in Chemistry and Math competitions at Mississippi College Competition (11-12)
- 6th in National Mu Alpha Theta Math Competition and 1st in Regional Competitions (11)
- 3rd in Federal Junior Duck Stamp Contest (9)

Essay

Science Rules

"Electricity rules!" roared a group of third graders, huddled around my display of light bulbs, hand-powered generators, static tubes, and other eye-luring gizmos. The place was hectic: over 1,200 elementary children grouped into ten or so, thrilled by the jerking of cloth with plates and glasses stacked on top; the tiny, swimming "bugs" seen only with a microscope; the number of water drops a nickel can hold; the vanishing of a cup of water; and other absorbing demonstrations.

I volunteered as a presenter at the MSMS Science Carnival not for recognition but instead, for my love of science. This passion sprouted from the long hours of scrutinizing posters of cell structures in my dad's laboratory during the summer. Only a fourth grader then, I was fascinated with the colorful double helix of DNA and was absorbed by the boldfaced words in books, sometimes too heavy for me to carry at once. With the vocabulary from a few introductory science classes, I embarked on reading some of those books and tried to digest as much of them.

My passion for science continued to blossom in high school when I dissected frogs, cats, and piglets to examine their anatomies; made ice cream to study Raoult's Law of freezing point depression; and mixed fake blood to analyze the compatibilities of each blood group. During the summers of my 9th and 10th grade years, I joined the extensive Jackson Heart Study, the first large-scale cardiovascular disease study in African-Americans to understand why they have a higher rate of heart disease and also enhance our overall knowledge of cardiovascular health.

I continued to satisfy my hunger for knowledge by attending the Mississippi School for Mathematics and Science, known for its rigorous academics. In addition to being challenged with Microbiology, AP Chemistry, and Adv. Physics in the 11th grade, I seized the opportunity to conduct research at Mississippi State University on the transport proteins that mediate detoxification processes in the mammalian kidney. *Loading buffers, agarose gels, and Polymerase Chain Reaction* quickly became my everyday vocabulary.

Research immediately became a favorite of mine. Last summer at the University Mississippi of Medical Center, I worked on several research projects on the vestibular system with laboratory rats. I helped with recording neuron activities of the locus cereulus to prove the synchronized bursts of neurons after injection of opiates such as morphine. To study the effects of labyrinthectomy on the vestibular system, I performed surgical techniques such as catheterization of the femoral artery to record blood pressure. I also started the project of recording the pupil movements of rats after unilateral and bilateral labyrinthectomies. This year at the College of Veterinary Medicine at MSU, I hope to develop a method to discover and characterize new herpes viruses using virus genomes from latently infected tissue - in our case from channel catfish infected with *Ictalurid herpesvirus*.

In addition to research, I am very thankful for the science forums including one with Dr. Claire Frasier, the president of The Institute of Genomic Research, and competitions such as *Science Bowl*, *Chemistry Olympiad*, and *Physics Olympiad*, in which I have been recognized at both the state and national levels. Because of the endless opportunities provided to make me who I am, I cherish sharing what I have learned. I do not mind being the host of chemistry and physics “parties” that sometimes last until three in the morning. I do not mind the children at the Science Carnival messing up my hair with static sticks. I do not mind shouting out my love for science with them. And I do not mind spending a day with children teaching them what I know-- and perhaps inspiring them to become future scientists, doctors, and engineers.

SECTION VII

UNIVERSITY OF PENNSYLVANIA

Official Name:	University of Pennsylvania
Location:	Philadelphia, PA 19104 USA
Website:	http://www.upenn.edu
Year established:	1740
Founder:	Benjamin Franklin
Motto:	*Leges Sine Moribus Vanae* "Laws without morals [are] useless"
Mascot:	The Quakers
Colors:	Red and Blue
Nicknames:	UPenn, Penn

Undergraduate student population:	10,275 (2008)
Freshmen population:	2,430 (2008)
Domestic students:	90%
International students:	10%

Colleges on campus:

The College at Penn (School of Arts and Sciences)
School of Engineering and Applied Science
School of Nursing
The Wharton School

Section editor: Xi "Sissi" Chen

Xi "Sissi" Chen

From Clarke Central to UPenn

High School

Clarke Central High School
350 S. Milledge Ave
Athens, GA 30605-1048

Population of Graduating Class: 298

Students to Ivy League Colleges that Year: 1

Extra-Curricular Activities During High School

Music/Arts

- High School Orchestra: Section leader (9-10) Concert Master (11)
- Athens String Ensemble (9-11)

Sports

- J.V. Volleyball: Starting player (9)
- Varsity Volleyball (10-12): Starting Player (12) Region Champions (12)
- Varsity Swimming (9-12): Practice Leader (9-11) Captain (12)
- Dolphin's Swim Team (9-11): Placed at State

Leadership

- Student Government Association (9-12): Vice President (12)
- National Honor's Society (10-12): Vice President (12)

- National Beta Club (10-12): Vice President (11), President (12)
- International Club (10-12): President (11-12)
- Academic Team (9-12)
- Math Team (11-12):
  Co-Founder (11)
  Co-Captain (11-12)
- Mock Trial: Region Champions (9-12):
  State Top 4 Finalists (9-12)

Volunteer Experience

- Emory Chinese School (11-12): Teacher's Aid
- Habitat for Humanity (10-11): Help build houses for low income families
- YMCA (9-10): Volunteer Swim Instructor
- Dolphins Swim Club (11-12): Volunteer Swim Coach
- Clarke Central High School ('10-12): After-School Tutor
- National Beta Club (10-12): President and responsible for organizing group volunteer events around the community
- National Honor's Society (10-12): Participated/ organized in monthly volunteer activities

Work Experience

- YMCA (10-12): Lifeguard and Swim instructor

Honors/Awards

- National Merit Scholar (12)
- Michelle Kwan Chevrolet REWARDS: Selected as 1 of 10 female athletes in the U.S. with strong athletic and academic performances in High School (12)
- Yale Book Award (11)
- Governor's Honor's Program in Math (11)
- Georgia Certificate of Merit (11)
- Hugh O'Brien Youth Leadership:
  Selected as one of the top 10th graders in GA to go to the HOBY Seminar (10)
- Phi Kappa Phi Honor Society: Award for Highest GHP in my grade (11)
- Who's Who Among American H.S. Students (9-12): Selected for 3 years in a row

- Who's Who Among American H.S. Athletes (2006)
- Athens Youth Leadership: Selected to participate in Athens Youth Leadership (11)
- Clarke Central High School:
  Teacher Honor Award (9)
  All A's Honor Roll (9-12)
  Athletic Scholar Award – selected as 4 year-Varsity Athlete with highest GPA

Essay

Question:
You are writing a 300 page Auto-biography. Please submit Page 263

Page 263 of My Auto-biography

my racing heart. I had to calm down because I knew the more nervous I am the worse I will swim. I fidgeted with my cap and goggles, hoping that neither would break once I dive into the water. I had a mental image of myself swimming with a leaking goggle, struggling to see and swim with water stinging my eyes at the same time. I stood behind the backstroker when our heat was called and I could hear the deafening pounding of my heart as I anxiously awaited my turn. I step onto the blocks and made final adjustments to my goggles. I took them off, wiped off the steam, adjusted them, took them off again, wiped of more fog, and put them back on, praying now that they won't fail me. I slowly bend down with my arms outstretched, tracking in the backstroker.

Swish! I enter the water in a smooth dive and mentally sigh in relief that I had not false started or lost my goggles. I do my underwater pullout and turn my full concentration onto the completion of my strokes as I begin to swim. Up and down, and up and down my head bobs as I breathe and I see the side of the pool nearing. I can hear my teammates yelling "go....go...go!" every time my head is above the water. I use their excitement and try to focus all my energy swimming as fast as I can. I completely forget all the pointers my coaches gave me about my form and technique. I'm too busy racing the other people to care if my strokes look pretty or not. Finally the end is within arms reach and I stretch myself out as far as I can with my eyes closed, reaching for the wall in one long stroke.

I quickly hop out of the pool and turn my attention on cheering our final swimmer on. Unable to yell too much between gasps, I bend down to catch my breath and mentally will our last swimmer to win the heat for us. The next I know, my teammates start jumping up for we had just won our heat, and we all race to the score sheets to anxiously await the final results. We placed Third! We were ecstatic and couldn't wait to share the news with our parents. As my teammates ran off to spread the joy, my pace slowed as I smiled and reflected on my personal accomplishments. Sure I'm glad that we won Third in State, but what I was more excited about was that I made it through my first State event in one piece. Considering the fact that I had joined the team just that summer, I was pretty proud just to have won District, and not messed up things at State. I had overcome my inexperienced 10-year-old nerves and swam the best swim I could hope for. There were two more events left that day, but they didn't really matter anymore. I had crossed the bridge and now I am unstoppable. If I can do it once, I can surely do it again. I had surmounted my anxiety and nothing else really matter anymore.

That night at the awards ceremony, I had never felt so excited. There was going to be a

Lilly Yeh

From Marple Newtown to UPenn

High School

Marple Newtown Senior High School
Newton Square, PA

Population of Graduating Class: 297

Students to Ivy League Colleges that Year: 4

Extra-curricular Activities During High School

Music/Arts

- Orchestra: Viola, Secretary
- Choir: Secretary

Leadership/Awards

- Interact Community Service Club: Co-President
- Hi-Q Academic Bowl
- National Honor's Society
- Renaissance Board
  Rewarded students for doing well in school with privileges, i.e. being able to do other activities during study hall

Sports

- Tennis team, Co-Captain

Volunteer Experience

- Interact Community Service Club, Co-President
- Franklin Institute Museum of Science, Volunteer
- National Honor Society, Tutoring/Mentoring

Essay

Personal Statement

I have been following the University of Pennsylvania almost as a duckling follows the first thing it sees. When I was in fifth grade, the daughter of a close family friend went there. Ever since then I have wanted to go to the University of Pennsylvania. I must admit that at the age of ten, I did not know of any colleges besides this one. However, as I have grown older and learned about more schools, this particular one has remained at the top of my list. Many people I know have gone to the University of Pennsylvania and have made it a model for me. As this university has become my aspiration, almost everything I have done in school and sometimes out of school has been accomplished with the goal of getting into the University of Pennsylvania.

The University of Pennsylvania also has certain characteristics that make it very appealing to me. It is a great school held in very high esteem. Its location, diversity, and flexibility also make the University of Pennsylvania perfect for me.

Located in the heart of Philadelphia, the University of Pennsylvania is only about thirty minutes from my home. It is close enough for periodic visits home and far enough to avoid seeing my family more than I really want to. The University of Pennsylvania is also located in a setting which to me seems ideal. It is located in an urban setting, but also has its own college campus feel. So, even though it is so close to home, it is in an entirely different environment than the one I have lived in my entire life.

As a minority, diversity is very important to me. Having lived in a predominantly white community, when I go to college I want to meet people of many different races, cultures, and backgrounds. I want to be able to meet people who are totally opposite of what I am and people who are just like me. I want to be able to find a place where I belong. Living in an environment with a diversity of people will open up my mind more and let me experience many different kinds of friendships. Penn, with its diversity, seems like a great place for that.

Academically, I am not sure what I wish to pursue at the moment. I only know I want to apply myself in science or math, since I have always enjoyed and excelled in both subjects. Bioengineering seems like a very attractive option to me right now and I have found that the University of Pennsylvania has a very good bioengineering program. I have also found a computational biology program that seems very interesting. Since these are only possible interests, the University of Pennsylvania's flexibility is very appealing to me. The flexibility of the programs makes the decisions I make now less pressured since I know I can change what I want to do later if what I have chosen doesn't fulfill my goals.

I love the University of Pennsylvania, for the reasons stated earlier and just because of the feel I get when I am standing on the campus. I can imagine myself walking down the streets, sitting in my room, and studying in the library as a student there at the University of Pennsylvania. I am very eager to go to college, and I hope that one year from right now, I will be living on the campus as a proud student of the University of Pennsylvania.

Jacinda Li

From Churchill to UPenn

High School

Winston Churchill
High School
11300 Gainsborough Road
Potomac, MD 20854

Population of Graduating
Class: 550

Students to Ivy
League Colleges that Year: 15

Extra-curricular Activities During High School

Music/Arts

- Modeling and Acting (9-12)
  Published in mid-Atlantic region magazine
  Worked in fashion shows for Seventeen Magazine, Macy's, Montgomery Mall
  Work with photographers on individual projects
  Acted in Pentagon Industrial Film

Leadership

- Churchill Forensics Public Speaking Team (9-12)
  Team Captain
- Biology Club (11-12), President
- Churchill National Honors Society (11-12)
  Tutor students in any subject
- Science National Honors Society (10-12)
  Fundraising Committee Chair
- French Honors Society (10-12)

Tutor students in French; Coordinate cultural activities; Conduct fundraisers; Increased tutoring efficiency by developing a reward system

Sports

- Churchill Basketball Team (9-10): Bulldog Award for the most dedicated and altruistic player
- Churchill Softball Team (10)
- AAU Maryland Flames Basketball Team (8-10) Highly competitive pre-professional team; Competed in tournaments in DC, Virginia, Maryland area.

Community Service/Volunteer Activities

- Arc of Montgomery County (9-12):
  Jr. Volunteer Coordinator
  Founder, Editor, Writer of Jr. Volunteer Newsletter
  Creator and Teacher of Healthy Living Courses
  Gymnastic Trainer
- Montgomery County Government (10-12)
  Appointed by County Executive; Advise schools and the County on policies concerning teens violence, drugs and alcohol, and discrimination; Organize county-wide educational student events such as "Battle of the Band," "Chalk out the Smoke," and "Gang Forum."
- Potomac Chinese School (10-12)
  Chief Executive of Student Government;
  Planned and Directed Chinese New Year Show; Won 1st Place in Chinese Speech Contest.
- Suburban Hospital (Summer, 10)
  Assisted Nutritionists in patients' dietetic management, staffed coffee cart for patients
- Churchill Guidance Office (Summer, 10)
  Filed documents, handled phone calls, assisted visitors in the counseling office.

Work Experience

- Modeling and Acting (10-12)
  Published in mid-Atlantic region magazine
  Worked in fashion shows for Seventeen Magazine, Macy's, Montgomery Mall

Work with photographers on individual projects
Acted in Pentagon Industrial Film

- Student Intern, Montgomery County Executive Government, Office of Community Outreach (11)
- Summer Intern (11), Medical and Clinical Psychology, Uniformed Service University of the Health Sciences
- Tutoring (10)

Honors/Awards

- Maryland Distinguished Scholar Finalist (11)
- National Youth Leadership Forum on Law Nominee (11)
- Outstanding Student in Psychology (11, given by the American Psychological Association)
- The Senate of Maryland Academic Achievement Award for students with Straight As (9, 11; given by Senator Rob Garagiola)
- Straight A Honor Roll (9-12, given by Churchill High School)
- 1st Place, Chinese American Youth Leadership and Service Award by Washington China Post (11)
- 1st Place, Public Speech Competition (11, given by Washington Metropolitan Association
- Semi-finalist, U.S.A. Biology Olympiad Competition 2006 (Given by Center for Excellence in Education)
- Forensics Public Speaking Tournament Champion 2006 (given by Montgomery County Forensics League
- National award for students with academic excellence (11, given by National Society of High School)
- National Honor Roll (9,11; given by National Honor Roll)
- The President's Volunteer Service Award (9-11, Given by The President's Volunteer Service Award)
- Outstanding Volunteer (9-11, given by The Arc of Montgomery County)
- Bulldog Award 2005 (given by Churchill Basketball Team)

- Who's Who Among American High School Students (Awarded to top 5% of nation's high school students)

Essay

The Life of a Model-Student

Perched on a rock with my emerald tail trailing underwater, I dramatically fling about the drape of black seaweed that is my hair. Water droplets trickle down where skin blends into scales. My radiant energy captures an audience that gathers to stare and even whistle. Smiling brightly, I savor the delicious delight in provoking passersby into absorbing the excitement that I express.

"That's a wrap," calls my photographer as he lowers his massive camera. His cue snaps me back into reality: I am not actually a mermaid, but a teenage model posing for a magazine photo-shoot inside a public water fountain in Washington D.C.

Modeling is a passion that I would never relinquish even after facing disapproval and scorn. "You mortify us," upbraid my parents, who uphold the Chinese and Japanese values of modesty. "Our co-worker spotted you in a show, and advised us to restrain you!" Despite such discouragements, I still cherish each fashion show and photo-shoot moment, when I can unleash raw emotions and fantasy. I worry, nevertheless, that people will not respect me in serious academic settings. With any luck, neither schoolmates nor teachers will find me in malls or magazines, and instead remain unaware of my extravagant double-life.

My luck expires during this photo-shoot.

The moment I playfully plunk into the fountain, I suddenly spot my teammate from my school's Forensics Public Speaking Team gawking at me disbelievingly. Imagine what an absurdity she sees: that studious captain, who drills her weekly on speeches about gun control, caught splashing around in a public fountain—in a fish suit! To salvage my reputation, I frantically seek refuge from her eyes, but where can I possibly hide when trapped half-naked? I shrink shamefully underwater until she walks away ... and hopefully develops amnesia.

During the following Forensics practice, I can hardly meet my teammate's knowing eyes. I inch over to her desk and force out a calm voice, "Let's practice your speech ..."

"You're a model?!"

Oh no, she remembers. As we drill through routines, I brace myself for the dirty looks and contemptuous scoffs that I often receive from Chinese elders. This time, however, the assaults do not come. Rather, my teammate seems to pay more attention to my coaching than usual.

Grateful yet curious, I ask, "You still have respect for me after finding out that I model? Don't you think models are pretentious and despicable?"

"No! You're so brave to let people watch and judge you like that."

Brave ...

I realize then that being a model is not shameful, but beneficial. Modeling gives me my courage—my willingness to face scrutiny and ridicule—that fuels other endeavors such as dramatizing in speech tournaments, in English or other languages. The exposure of my double-life is not a debacle, but a most liberating and empowering experience. From now on, the flamboyant model side of me will no longer hide like a mermaid hides from fishermen. I will greet all other "You're a model?" inquiries with luminous smiles.

SECTION VIII

YALE UNIVERSITY

Official Name:	Yale University
Location:	New Haven, Connecticut
Website:	http://www.yale.edu
Year established:	1701
Founders:	Founded by colonial clergymen and named after Elihu Yale
Motto:	*Lux et veritas* "Light and truth"
Mascot:	Bulldogs (Handsome Dan)
Color:	Blue

Undergraduate student population:	5,247 (2009)
Freshmen population:	1,308 (2009)
Domestic students	92%
International students:	8%

Colleges on campus:
Yale College
Graduate School of Arts and Sciences
10 Professional Schools: Architecture, Art, Divinity, Drama, Forestry and Environmental Studies, Law, Management, Medicine, Music, Nursing, and Public Health

Section editor: Lynn Wang

Lynn Wang

From Whitney to Yale

High School

Whitney High School
16800 Shoemaker Ave.
Cerritos, CA 90703

Population of Graduating Class: 179

Students to Ivy League Colleges that Year: 5

Extra-curricular Activities During High School

Sports

- Varsity Girls Tennis (10-12)
- Varsity Track and Field (9)

Music

- School choir accompanist (9)

Publications

- School newspaper *Aspects* (10-12)
  Features section editor (12)
  Focus section editor (11)
  Staff writer (10)
- Class of '07 Inner Council Director of newsletters (11)

Community Service/Volunteer Activities

- Chinese American Teach Abroad Program Founder/Executive Director (11-12)
- PingAn Acupuncture Clinic, Volunteer (12)
- Rancho Los Amigos National Rehabilitation Center, Volunteer/Assistant Researcher (10)

Leadership/Clubs

- Chinese American Teach Abroad Program-Whitney High School Club President (11-12)
- Model United Nations (9-12)
  Undersecretary-General of Finance (12)
- Future Business Leaders of America
  President (11)
  Secretary of Communication and Internal Operations (10)
- Melodia (a musical community service club)
  Secretary (11)
- California Scholastic Federation (10-12)
- California Junior Scholastic Federation (9)
- National Honor Society (12)

Work Experience

- Maritz Research, Bilingual Telephone Interviewer (11-12)
- District Office of Congresswoman Linda Sanchez, Spring Intern (11)
- Whitney High School Learning Center Tutor (10)

Honors/Awards

- Class of 2007 Valedictorian (12)
- AP National Scholar (12)
- Presidential Scholar Semifinalist (12)
- National Merit Scholarship (12)
- California Scholastic Federation Seal-bearer (12)
- Joseph Cho Scholarship (11)
- Minor in Business Administration from Cerritos College (11)
- Maritz Research Model New Employee Award (12)
- Who's Who in California High School Students (10)
- Varsity Girls Tennis Team Singles MVP (11)
- Certificate of Merit Level Advanced from the Music Teachers' Association of California (9)

Others

- CACC Summer Program, Participant (9)
- Ran the 2006 Los Angeles Marathon and placed in top quartile of age group (11)

Essay

A Whole New World

I quietly sat in the back row during class, overwhelmed by the gibberish around me. At lunch, I stood alone against a brick wall, enviously watching groups of giggling children playing and making strange noises. I listened for words, but heard only sounds. I spoke, but only received quizzical stares from others. In just a few days, I had tumbled from class president to social outcast.

This transformation came about when I was a seven-year-old in second grade, and my family moved from Urumuqi, China to Sydney, Australia. After my miserable first day at Campsie Elementary School ended, I dashed to my parents in relief—finally, two people who understood me! Still, I arrived home in tears of anguish.

The next morning, I ate breakfast with a silent dread. Sympathizing with my horrid experience from the previous day, my mom gently asked me, "Do you still want to go to school today?" Expecting a "no," she stopped short of persuading me to go when I surprised her with a firm "yes."

Back then, I did not understand the reason for my response because it was completely against my feelings. Now, I realize that my reply stemmed from my deep desire to learn. Only by going to school could I continue to learn. Thus, I saw no other options.

No matter how much I feared school at first, I faced it head-on. The more isolated I felt, the harder I worked to make up for my deficiency. My parents, who were fluent in English, taught me new words everyday and tested me regularly. To improve my pronunciation, I read story books out loud, and memorized and recited some of my favorites, like the one about a talking bear that appeared in a girl's house and used her shampoo without asking. Even now, I can still vividly recall the exact words she used to describe her reaction: "This is not acceptable!"

In the evenings, I desperately wanted to join my family in watching Chinese dramas, but instead, I sat alone in my bedroom, completing reading comprehension exercises from a gray workbook I borrowed from the library. Determined to conquer the language barrier as fast as possible, I even muttered English words in my sleep, as my grandparents later told me.

After a month of effort, my ESL teacher Mrs. Bransgrove gave me an award for "trying hard to learn English." It motivated me to work even harder and learn faster, and in a record-setting eight months, I graduated from ESL. Attending regular class for the first time was thrilling; even though I still couldn't understand everything I heard, I could at least grasp an idea of what was going on around me. No longer a lost foreigner, I eventually summoned enough courage to approach my classmates, talk to them, and make new friends. As I lost my fear, school became the exciting place it had once been in China.

In the following year, my classmates elected me to Student Council. Nothing could contain my ecstatic pride when I walked across the stage in the inaugural ceremony to receive my badge as a "Student Councilor." To my further delight, the New South Wales Parliament mailed me a certificate of "Achievement and Responsibility" for being elected to this position. Carefully, I taped the precious piece of paper to my bedroom wall. It had taken a year, but I was once again a leader among my peers.

Today, the certificate is still on display in my bedroom. I brought it to America as a keepsake and properly framed it here. Although it may seem small when compared with my more recent achievements, it reminds me of my struggles and triumph at an early age, before I even understood my motivation to learn. It reminds me that no matter how difficult the situation may be, I will prevail so long as I put forth my best.

Jack Li

From Jersey Village to Yale

High School

Jersey Village High School
7600 Solomon Street
Houston, Texas 77040

Population of Graduating Class: 820

Students to Ivy League Colleges that Year: 1

Extra-curricular Activities During High School

Music/Arts

- School Symphonic Concert Band (9-12), Principle Bassoon
- School Concert Orchestra (9-12), Principle Bassoon
- Varsity Marching Band (9-12), Drum Major (12)
- Houston Youth Orchestra (10), Principle Bassoon

Publications

- School Literary Magazine, In Flight, "The Restaurant," Houston, Texas 2008

Community Service/Volunteer Activities

- Memorial Hermann Hospital Volunteer (10-12)
- Member of Texas Association of Auxiliary Volunteers (11-12)

Clubs/Leadership

- Spanish Club (10-12), President (11)
- Rotary Interact Club (9-12), Vice President (12)
- Literary Criticism Team (12)

Work Experience

- China Bear Chinese Buffet (12), Waiter
- Kumon Learning Center (12), Tutor

Honors/Awards

- National Honor Society (11-12)
- Spanish National Honor Society (10-12)
- AP Scholar
- Bill Archer Internship (11), Finalist

Others

- Love to play basketball and weight lifting

Essay

Only Son

At the end of my junior year I was broke. Not broke as in I've run out of money, rather I've never had money. The truth was that at age seventeen, I had never held a steady job before. My parents have always been kind to me, so a job had never been a necessity, but as I grew older, guilt always accompanied my parents' charity. Besides, I'd been looking forward to having a little bit of money at my disposal to spend freely (and possibly wastefully). So it was decided; I was going to finally get a job. After looking into a few fast food places and deciding that I'd rather get paid, I asked my mom if I can work with her at China Bear Chinese Buffet. What I sought was a summer job to earn a little extra cash; what I found was a deeper understanding, sincere appreciation, and absolute respect for my mother.

The first day of work I was more than confident: what could be so hard about waiting tables? The job description was simple: bring the customers their drinks, clear the table when they're done, give them their check, and make sure they pay. If I could memorize all the special trig functions and burst out with more than sixty steps of photosynthesis on command, I thought, the restaurant will "be nothing but a chicken wing." Besides, mom had worked there for ten years; if she could do it, so could I.

> *New customer table three, better go check what drinks they want. Just three drinks, easy enough. Here you go, sir, enjoy! Better look around. Dirty plates on tables four and five; should clean those before they pile up. Oh, look, new customers table eight. Let me go check what drinks they want and then take the plates so I don't have to make two trips to the station. Let me take those plates from you, sir. Here are your drinks ma'am, enjoy!*

By midday I was feeling the pain. My arms ached from carrying plates, my feet agonized from ceaseless walking and standing, but worst of all, my patience wore thin as I dealt with each customer, all of whom were determined to make my life just a bit harder. I soon found out that working as a waiter meant dealing with an amazing array of difficult customers, most of whom could be easily identified. There were the benchwarmers, who sat at a table for hours just taking up space. There were the complainers and demanders, who cannot seem to eat all by themselves. There were the much despised tight-purses, who shamelessly leave little tip, no tip, or negative tip (by running out on the bill and thereby making it the unfortunate waiter's responsibility). The worst, however, in my eyes were the food-wasters who grab a whole plate of precious (and expensive) food only to realize that they do not like it. Growing up reciting children's rhymes that taught me that "each grain of rice was made from a bead of a farmer's sweat," it hurt me personally to see the shiny white rice, the golden baby corn, and the succulent sweet and sour chicken dumped into the trash. Yet this was a scene repeated at every table, and these customers kept coming back every day. The result of one such customer was frustration; the result of many was insanity. *So why does she keep working here?*

> *Where's that pitcher? I've got to refill the cokes. Here you go sir. Oh really? I apologize I didn't realize you had Dr. Pepper I'll get another glass for you I apologize again sir I'm very busy. Oh here comes a big party on table nine, eleven drinks I'd have to make three trips to the station! Fast fast fast. Yes ma'am I see those dirty plates I'll be right back to get them. Is a little patience too much to ask for and where IS that busboy if he doesn't clean eight and four no new customers can come in. Wait, has four paid yet?*

Closing time was the happiest of times. The drive home was silent; Mom and I were both much too tired to talk. When I arrived home, I promptly dropped into bed, my body ready to give up. As I lay there, I remembered the countless nights over the years when my mom had come home like this, ten, eleven, twelve o'clock at night. She would always tiptoe to my room to see if I were asleep. If I was awake, she would sit on the bed and ask me about my day. I remembered the times when I would get annoyed and tell her to go away because I was *tired*. I remembered the times when I pretended to be asleep so I wouldn't have to talk to her. She would look in through my door, and seeing me sleeping, would walk away disappointed. Funny, this little emotion of guilt; it is a combination of shame, regret, and self-abhorrence. It is suddenly gaining perspective that one somehow missed all the times before. Didn't I know that she had worked all day and that *she* was the tired one? Could I have missed the fact that, because of our schedule, this was the *only* time during the day, and sometimes during the whole week that she gets to see her son? Was I too selfish to realize she had worked ten years and never taken a single vacation? Have I grown so prodigal that I forget that my fancy computer, brand name clothes, my shiny sports shoes were a product of her endless hard work and toil? No, I did not sleep that night, I couldn't. I had work the next day. Should I go? Could I put up with the endless walking and rude customers again? Yes, mom had worked there for ten years; if she could do it, so could I.

They say to really know someone, one has to walk a mile in his or her shoes. Well, after the many (many many!) miles I shared with my mother that summer in the restaurant fetching drinks and clearing plates, I've grown to have a much clearer understanding of the depth of her strength and the power of her love. A thought that had buoyed my spirit after dealing with a particularly nasty customer was the idea that this was just a temporary job, that I could walk away from this restaurant and never come back. Unfortunately, this is not the case for my mom, and for most people working at these restaurants. They are tired people, dragging their unwilling bodies thirteen hours a day, completing tasks they despise, working a job they have no passion for. So why continue? China Bear is not any different from any of the thousands of restaurants across the United States, and the men and women, including my mother, are not any different from the thousands working elsewhere. They seem to melt into one mass, a generation of men and women with the same thoughts, same desires, and same dreams. *Only Son, you must go to college so you don't live as we do.* And so they work.

There is no way to sufficiently demonstrate my appreciation for all that my mother has done for me. For starters, I never ask her for anything profligate again. I cherish every moment I could spend with her and thank her for every meal she has time to cook for me. Oh, and now I can no longer sleep unless I've waited for my mom to come home, so I can asked her about her day. I can tell from her smile that she appreciates my change. I can tell from her smile that she knows I finally understand.

Only Son, you must go to college so you don't live as we do.

Chi Wing "Jessica" Qu

From Lowell to Yale

High School

Lowell High School
1101 Eucalyptus Dr.
San Francisco, CA 94132

Population of Graduating Class:
650

Students to Ivy
League Colleges that Year: 10

Extra-curricular Activities During High School

Sports

- Lowell Dragon Boat Team (10-12)

Music/Arts

- Violinist and Pianist, UC Berkeley Young Musicians Program (11-12)
- Co-Concert Master, Lowell Symphony Orchestra and String Quartet (10-12)
- Violinist, All-City Honored Festival Orchestra (10, 11)

Publications

- Reporter, "The Lowell" Newspaper Team (10-12)

Leadership/Community Service

- President, Youth Accelerates Youth (YAY) Outreach Program (10-12)
- Community Liaison, American Red Cross Youth Service Team (9-12)
- President, Lowell Volunteers Club (10-11)

- Member, Shield and Scroll Honor and Service Society (11-12)

Clubs

- Member, Lowell Forensics Society (10-12)
- Student Representative, Academic Affairs Committee (9-12)
- Member, California Scholarship Federation (10-12)

Work Experience

- Intern, Chinese Historical Society of America Internship Program (Summer of 9)
- Summer Camp Counselor, Cameron House Youth Ministry Program (Summer of 10)

Honors/Awards

- Gates Millennium Scholar (12)
- Coca-Cola Scholar (12)
- President's Service Award (11)
- Broad Prize for Urban Education Scholar (12)
- AP Scholar with Honor (12)
- The Violet Richardson Service Award (11)
- National Forensics League Degree of Excellence (11)
- Certification of Distinction in Piano and Music Theory from The Associated Board of Royal Schools of Music, England (11)
- Miss Teen Chinatown Princess (10)

Others

- Proficiency in reading and writing Chinese
- Native Fluency in speaking Cantonese, Mandarin, and Shanghainese

Essay

Finding My Voice

When I arrived in America five years ago, I was deaf and mute, figuratively speaking. My first trembling steps into my seventh-grade classroom were greeted with intimidating stares and whispers. Later, when I replied with a timid "I don't know" to my teacher's simple question, the class erupted into laughter. Embarrassed, I felt intense feelings of inadequacy welling up within me.

As a newly arrived immigrant, I felt uprooted and lost. However, I soon found a sense of direction, thanks to a free weekly tutoring program sponsored by a local non-profit organization. There, I met a person who was about to take on a pivotal role in my life — my tutor. She provided me with individual instruction on conversational English, grammar, and American culture and history. After much hard work, my English improved dramatically, and I had the distinction of being promoted out of ESL after only one year.

Overcoming the language barrier was an essential first step for me. Then, I was able to serve as a translator for my mother as she navigated the maze of paperwork and assistance programs established to help newly arrived immigrants. At the same time, I began to realize how many opportunities we had missed because we did not understand enough English at the outset. After experiencing this sense of isolation and helplessness, I was inspired to reach out to other immigrants and use my personal experience to facilitate their immigration process.

My participation in Youth Accelerates Youth (YAY) Outreach Program has allowed me to give back to my community in a meaningful way. As the YAY President, my goal is to help newly arrived immigrants to become productive, self-reliant, and contributing members of their communities. Our tutoring and mentoring programs have seen measurable improvement in the English reading, writing, and conversational skills of our students. In fact, our services have allowed both students and parents to communicate with school administrators and teachers in their native tongues and address concerns regarding school and assistance programs.

Looking back now, I realize how much my attitude and outlook on life changed when I found my "voice." I am no longer deaf and mute, but have learned to really listen to those around me and speak up without hesitation. Through my close interaction with my tutees, I have gained a deeper appreciation of each person's unique contribution to our great society. Furthermore, I have realized that my project's commitment to others has helped us to connect with what is best within ourselves. After all, making a difference in the world is not so difficult if one is willing to sacrifice a part of oneself to change the world for the better.

Joanna Cornell

From Wootton to Yale

High School

Thomas Sprigg Wootton
High School
2100 Wootton Parkway
Rockville, MD 20850

Population of Graduating
Class: 602

Students to Ivy
League Colleges that Year:
14

Extra-curricular Activities During High School

Music/Arts

- Classical Piano (K-12)
  Washington post Music & Dance Scholarship
  Finalist, 1st Place Miriam Shields Gottlieb
  Memorial Piano Competition
  1st Place Young Artist Competition
  1st Place Honors Audition
  1st Place Maryland State Music Teacher's
  Association Festival Piano Solo Competition

Community Service

- Earned over 1200 community service hours
  Montgomery County Historical Society (8-12)
  Summer Intern, Museum Docent
  Shady Grove Nursing Home (7-11)
  Lunchtime Tutoring (9-12)

Montgomery County Teen Court (9-11)

Leadership/Clubs

- Mock Trial Team (9-12), Captain
- Model UN (9-12), Fundraising Leader
- Foundation for Children of Atyrá (9-12), President
- National Spanish Honor Society (9-12), President
- Maryland Teenage Democrats (10-12), State Deputy Secretary, School Coordinator
- Student Homeroom Advisory Promotes Excellence (9-12)
- National Honor Society (11-12)
- National Science Honor Society (11-12)

Work Experience

- Peer2Peer Tutors (10-12)-Senior Manager
- Panera Bread, Co. (11-12)-Associate Trainer
- United States House of Representatives Page (11)
- Annapolis Senate Page (12)
- Summer Intern for Congresswoman Millender-McDonald (10)

Honors/Awards

- National Merit Winner (12)
- National AP Scholar, AP State Scholar (12)
- Pedram Tousi Hall of Fame Award (11)
- Marian Friendman Greenblatt Award for Excellence in Social Studies (11)
- Maryland Distinguished Scholar Finalist (12)
- Official Citation from the Senate of Maryland for Stellar Academic Achievement (9-12)

Essay

The Joy Luck Dumpling Club

Splish, splash, splish. The sound of dumplings landing in a giant pot of boiling water fills the room with excitement. In just a few moments, smells of cilantro, ginger, chive, pork, and chicken begin to drift across the room, making everyone's stomachs growl with eager anticipation. It is my favorite day of the month: dumpling day.

As a young child, I eagerly looked forward to that one weekend day that was dedicated to my favorite Chinese food, dumplings. Right after lunch, my parents, grandparents, and family friends would gather around our small, wooden kitchen table and make dumplings. The women would deftly cut out slices of thin, white dough, sprinkling flour on the bottom, and then adding chunks of meat, with an assortment of vegetables and spices, our own special recipe, to the dough. Like experts, they would then add drops of water along the sides, and fold the dough into a delicious-looking delicacy, all while animatedly chatting.

Meanwhile, the men would sit in the living room playing bridge. The other little kids and I were usually running around the house, screaming, without a care in the world. We would eagerly clamor around the kitchen, clutching our little stomachs and asking for food. The mothers and grandmothers would then laugh. Sometimes, my mother would even let me make a dumpling, but it would always come apart.

At dinner, everyone would pull up myriads of fold-up chairs and beat up bean bags to the table, eat, and tell stories. As I unskillfully dipped my dumplings into black vinegar and soy sauce, the adults at the table would tell work stories, discuss politics, and reminisce about the past, in a way similar to the scenes of Amy Tan's *The Joy Luck Club*. It was during these dinners, in which I truly understood the meaning of family, friendship, and community. All of the different families eating in my house shared one common food, tying us together in an unbreakable bond.

The warmth created by dumplings quickly changed when I moved from the small town of Lawrence, Kansas, to the DC metropolitan area. When my family and I first arrived, we were amazed by the wide variety of food in the local grocery stores. Suddenly, dumplings were omnipresent, sold at a cheap price of ten dollars for three bags, sometimes four if we were lucky. My parents were ecstatic, and week after week they eagerly filled our shopping carts with bags of dumplings, boiling them every weekend for lunch.

These store bought dumplings were supposed to be better than the homemade ones I used to eat. With machines, the dough could be thinner, the meat could be exactly proportioned, and the texture and look could be flawless. My parents thought these "perfect," store-bought dumplings would make us happy, but they were wrong. These dumplings were convenient, taking only ten minutes to cook, but failed to bring all of the different families together.

No longer did we have dumpling days, or any type of gathering involving dumplings. The dumplings were unceremoniously shoved to the back of my freezer, only to be taken out on weekends for a quick meal. Along with the absence of dumplings from big gatherings comes more change. Instead of light-hearted gossip, dinner parties seem to be dominated by more stressful topics such as SATs, grades, and piano competitions. And as I grow older, my weekends have become filled with endless activities, making it almost impossible for my family to plan weekly gatherings. As a result, my family now only hosts around three dinner parties a year, all without dumplings.

But despite these changes, I sometimes still see figments of those fond dumpling parties of my childhood. The little kids still run around the house, jumping on couches and screaming, until the parents complain about the excessive noise. And while I no longer join the little kids on their rampage, I now sit with the adults, chatting about my busy day at Panera, reminiscing about my summers on the Hill, celebrating the Mock Trial Team's recent victory, and listening to everyone else's stories.